# THE
# ART OF
# PAS DE DEUX

# THE
# ART OF
# PAS DE DEUX

## by Nicolai Serrebrenikov

Translated from
the Russian and with
additional technical material

by

## Joan Lawson

DANCE BOOKS LTD
9 Cecil Court, London WC2

First published 1978 by Dance Books Ltd.,
9 Cecil Court, London WC2N 4EZ.

Printed by The Burlington Press (Cambridge) Ltd.

ISBN 0 903102 46 3

# FOREWORD

In translating Serrebrenikov's book on partnering from the Russian I have felt it necessary to add some comment of my own to help those studying his lessons and exercises. I first practised *pas de deux* with my colleagues Anton Dolin and Keith Lester (whose first partner I was) in the studio of Seraphina Astafieva. Later I was privileged to study under that great teacher Agrippina Vaganova in Leningrad. Finally, as an onlooker and prospective teacher, I was allowed to watch Serrebrenikov's classes. I am therefore very aware of the infinite care and patience that is always taken when teaching such expertise.

I am also aware that, without adding something of the important and frequently humorous comment that this brilliant teacher gives to all participants in his class, not all his wise advice will be understood. He works, after all, with students who have already spent five years acquiring the firm technical background and basic principles of the Leningrad Choregraphic Academy, Vaganova, before they come to his lessons for the final three years of perfection which complete their eight year course. Before this they have not practised any form of classical *pas de deux*, although both boys and girls are used to working with each other in the folk, social and character dance lessons. Attempting any classical *pas de deux* before these students reach the three final years of training is considered unwise because the boys, in particular, are not allowed to undergo the physical strain of supporting a girl before they can control their spinal and leg muscles. Moreover, as children's growth can be spasmodic, and if they suddenly begin to grow before the age 15-16, then every precaution is taken to ensure, firstly: the girl with whom they dance is an appropriate height; secondly: she can support her own weight at all times by centering her balance correctly over her own foot or feet; and thirdly: no boy is allowed to lift any girl until growth either stops or is definitely slowing up, and he is able to control the full length and stretch of his spinal and leg muscles.

I am greatly indebted to Walter Trevor and Sara Neil, my colleagues at the Royal Ballet School, for working through all the examples for me. As erstwhile soloists and now teachers of the students there, they are fully aware of the difficulties of putting into words what is so infinitely much easier to do in practice, particularly when the words are in a foreign language and not all the terms are the same as those used in England.

JOAN LAWSON

3

# GLOSSARY

As some of the technical terms used may not be familiar to readers who have never worked in the Vaganova school, the following brief glossary may be of help.

*The numbering of the square:* see sketch 1

| *The positions of the arms* | *R.A.D.* | *Cecchetti* |
|---|---|---|
| Preparatory | *Bras bas* | 5th *en bas* |
| 1st | 1st | 5th *en avant* |
| 2nd | 2nd | 2nd |
| 3rd | 5th | 5th *en haut* |

All others are explained, e.g., right arm in 1st, left arm in 3rd.

*The positions of the feet*
These are the same in every school. However in double-work the boy and girl sometimes use 6th position, i.e., the feet are together as in 1st, but not turned-out so that the feet are parallel and both knees face front; see sketch 49.

*The four arabesques:* see sketch 6
*High arabesque:* see sketch 40
*Low arabesque:* see sketch 42

*Passé* is used instead of *retiré* and also when the working leg is bent and brought back to the supporting leg before being stretched outwards into another pose or *développé.*

*Tire-bouchon* is used when the working leg is brought upwards from 5th, *sur le cou de pied* or *low retiré* to the highest possible point whilst still bent.

*Glissade* is as performed in all schools, but can move from 5th to 4th, or from 4th to 4th before an *assemblé* or jump upwards.

*Pas glissade* usually means that the working foot stretches outwards strongly and momentarily pauses on the floor before springing up again. It is also used like a *pas glissé* into *tombé.*

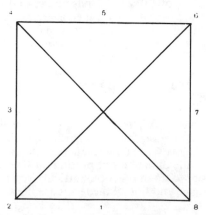

1. Numbering the plan. Dancer in the centre

# INTRODUCTION

In all *pas de deux*, both supported adage and lifts, the boy is not working with an automaton or a dead weight. The girl at all times is equally responsible for the performance and must be reminded to play her proper part, no matter how little, if the *pas de deux* is to convey the truth of the partnership between boy and girl.

Another important factor the teacher must take into consideration when introducing first-year students to double-work is to ensure that the partners are suitably matched for height and weight. This is particularly important when it is obvious that they are still growing. Although it would seem that the boy should be ideally half as heavy again as the girl, such a situation is rare at the age of 15-16 when study begins, but the girl's weight should always be less than the boy's. So should her height, even when she stands *sur les pointes*. It is also preferable if the length of the girl's legs and arms are well matched with the boy's. If they are extra long, or the boy's are short in comparison with the girl's, difficulties can arise in the first stages of training.

## RHYTHM

Firstly it is essential that the boy and girl understand and react to each other's rhythm. They must co-ordinate their movements by correct breathing, controlling it in such a way that it gives the greatest help to any movement from the simplest rise out of a *demi-plié* and *relevé sur les pointes* and from any position with and without a preparation to the highest possible lift or jump, the boy using only one hand.

## TEMPO

Secondly it is essential that both boy and girl understand and react to each other's tempo. This is largely dictated by the 'force' and/or impetus needed to perform some lift, turn, *pirouette* or other step and finally–and vitally–by their joint response to the music.

## FEELING AND HOLDING

The boy must also understand the subtle difference between 'feeling' the girl's movement and 'holding' her to maintain her equilibrium (see p. 6) as he lifts her in some position. He must 'feel' the tilt of her pelvis as she 'bows' over her leg in any *arabesque* and how it straightens when she returns to *rétiré*, or moves her leg in a *grand rond de jambe;* see p 12. He must 'feel' she is centrally balanced during a multiple *pirouette*, but when the *pirouette* finishes he must 'hold' her as firmly as he 'holds' her when he is lifting her on to his shoulder or during a simple *promenade*; see p 28.

## BREATHING

Breathing in all forms of *pas de deux* is all important. Both boy and girl must learn to breathe together deeply and by expanding the lungs, and thus the rib-cage, outwards and inwards sideways. For this reason the boy's hands must never press on to the girl's lower ribs (see p. 9). Both boy and girl must always breathe in with the effort and always through the nose, using all three parts of their lungs so that the rib-cage expands and contracts sideways and not up and down. It is also important to understand the exact timing of the breath.

*Example:* to the sound of the two syllables 'P–F' expel as much air as those syllables allow; pause a moment; then breathe in deeply and repeat this exercise several times. Later change the timing of the pause and breath. Then use this method during all the exercises quoted later, where it will be found that the quick breathing out after the effort has been made and the slight pause before breathing in again allows the pose attained to be firmly held.

## CORRECT PLACING
Both boy and girl must take the correct stance and understand where the central line of balance runs through both their bodies and in relationship to their work together. They must also understand how to counterbalance (counterpoise) each other's movements to maintain equilibrium by knowing the rules of balance, particularly the law of opposition; see p 7.

> Movement made by any dancer can be symmetrical or asymmetrical. In pure classical dance symmetry is demanded.
> —*Dame Ninette de Valois*

a. The normal body is naturally symmetrical. The arms and legs are balanced equally on each side of the body. The crown of the head is directly centred over the feet. The weight of the body is thus equally distributed over a firm base. It is important that the boy realises that, as soon as he raises the girl even slightly from the floor, if only on to her *pointes*, he must keep her weight centred as well as his own over his own foot or feet. He must also realise that once he and his partner achieve turn-out, the weight of his as well as her body must remain firmly centred over that base, even though it has changed shape and will grow less, particularly when the weight is transferred over to the girl's one foot and she has risen *sur la pointe*.

It is because the classical dancer has to use the turn-out that the spine must be strengthened from the earliest stage of training. But it is also essential that in *pas de deux* the boy is helping the girl to balance, and particularly when lifting her in any way from the floor, therefore, he must not use the full turn-out in any circumstances (see p. 10). He MUST keep his own weight firmly centred over as broad a base as possible. If he uses the turn-out in its complete form, his weight is certain to fall too far back when he lifts the girl from the floor. Therefore although the terms 1st, 2nd, 4th and 5th positions are used throughout this book, as far as the boy is concerned these are only approximate and are not technically correct as they must be when he is dancing a solo. The sketches clearly show the degree of turn-out most useful.

b. In order to keep the head and body correctly placed in relationship to the legs, the spine must be held firmly, but not stiffened. Its natural curves, from the waist upwards, MUST continue to act as shock-absorbers as they do naturally. They must allow both boy and girl to make the necessary adjustments of balance in every change of weight.

## FOUR IMPORTANT RULES

1. Each part of a limb and the body must be kept in natural relationship to the other and to the central line of balance.

2. Never allow the arm or leg to over- or under-cross the central line. This is most important for the boy when lifting the girl to his shoulder or chest.

3. The head, being the heaviest part of the body, must always lead the movement. The foot or feet must always find the head. The head never finds the feet, that is, the head always anticipates the movement and the direction to be taken.

4. The arms must never fall behind the body or shoulders. If they do, the weight will be too far back.

N.B. There are some modern lifts that do require the arms behind the shoulders, but in these cases careful attention must be paid to find the correct counterpoise and pull of force between the boy and his partner.

## THE LAWS OF BALANCE

There are only two laws of balance which have to be memorised and used appropriately when following the line of dance.

### 1. The Law of Opposition

Always use the opposite arm forwards to leg in front, whether it is working or supporting. When using this law, the girl and boy must be in the correct alignment, i.e., with hips and shoulders level lying parallel to each other and facing the same plane, and directed to one point in the square; see sketch 1. The boy's and girl's central line of balance must be seen to be at an equal distance from the other's from the crown of the head to the base. This rule is very important at the beginning of training.

### 2. The Law of Epaulement

Whether the forward leg is working or supporting, always bring the corresponding shoulder forwards. This rule is usually employed when a movement requires to be 'shaded' as in certain romantic ballets and modern lifts.

a. Whichever rule is used, both partners must decide the relationship of the arms and legs to the central line of balance and see that the opposition or *épaulement* used is logical, remembering that the central line of balance may lie between their two bodies (in supported adage), or through the boy's body and legs as he lifts the girl. The teacher should then ask the girl and boy the following questions:

7

Is the weight correctly centred?

Are the arms and legs so counterpoised that they help to maintain balance?

Do the opposing forces of arms and legs equalise the pressure of weight on the supporting legs (leg)? (*see sketch* 49).

Does this position help the dancers to remain calm and hold the pose?

Is it easy to move from that step or pose to another as the weight is transferred without twisting some part of the body, thus spoiling the line of movement?

b. The weight of the body must be equally distributed throughout, particularly in such poses when the girl is in *attitude* or *arabesque*, when she must tilt or bow her pelvis over the supporting leg as the working leg is raised or stretched behind. She must elongate her lower spine and leg and stretch the upper spine, curving it backwards towards the centre.

N.B. Her arms only add to the total picture by complementing that line.

c. The middle of the body (i.e., the centre of the waist) is the central part of both the boy's and girl's personal cube. The legs and arms can be directed to the edges, the tips of the fingers and toes being the extreme limits of those lines running diagonally through the body in two directions. Therefore the arms and legs must be raised or lowered in relation to the movements made outwards from the centre.

d. The pull between the opposing forces of arms and legs helps the dancers to maintain balance. But this can only be achieved if the partners make a strong movement with the arms and an intake of breath so that they begin and end with the movement of the legs, and do so simultaneously.

e. A most important rule for the girl in double-work of all kinds is to get into a position and hold it until both she and her partner have completed the movement or lift.

# PART I

## BASIC HOLDS IN SUPPORTED ADAGE

1. Two hands on the waist with elbows and wrists held downwards. The correct placing of the boy's hands during the first lessons in supported adage is all important. The sides of the wrist are held downwards, the palm and the four fingers held firmly on the sides of the girl's body at waist level. The little finger rests above the hip and the thumb is stretched slightly upwards resting firmly on the large spinal muscles. The girl MUST cultivate and hold her waistline firm at all times. On no account must the boy grasp the girl's lower ribs, or so spread his fingers that they dig into her flesh. Nor at any time must his hands or fingers slip upwards to touch or pinch her breasts; see sketch 2.
2. Two hands on wrists, or arms, or the partners hand in hand with palms together; the boy's hand over or under the girl's and other grasps; see sketch 23.
3. One hand on the waist, wrist, arm or hand in hand.
4. Cradle hold. Boy's arm circled round the girl's body either under or over in some way; see sketch 47.

All these holds should be practised using:

1. Static positions, i.e., without travelling and with or without preparations in *demi-plié* or *fondu*.
2. Moving from pose to pose through *passé, grand rond de jambe en dehors* and *en dedans*, etc.
3. Changing from pose to pose with a change of weight or passing step.
4. Poses, the boy using *promenade* in some part or a whole circle.
5. Poses turning the girl with and without *ports de bras* and with or without the girl circling her body.
6. The girl returning to the boy from one to another or the same pose; see p 12.
7. Boy and girl coming towards each other with one step or another. In these cases each must know the length of their own step and whether it is to be taken from straight legs or from *demi-plié* or *fondu*.

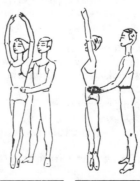

2. *Relevé* in 5th, and the boy's position behind the girl

The boy must anticipate exactly where the girl's centre of balance will lie when standing on her *pointe* or *pointes* in any pose and in various transfers of weight as she moves, whether to a pose or *à terre*. This centring of weight is vital to every aspect of partnering.

During the first lessons concentration must be made on the principles of partnering before any attempt is made to lift the girl into the air. The teacher should create as many varied *enchaînements* as possible within the capacity of his students to give them freedom to adapt to each other's movements.

Although it is recommended that during first lessons in double-work the boy should stand behind the girl in a not too wide 2nd position and never fully turned-out, it is useful for him also to practise in an open 4th position where the front foot is mid-way between a true 4th and 2nd. This position is invaluable later for *pirouettes* with some girls (see p. 18). The boy must at all times ensure that the central line of balance through his own legs is absolutely correct, whether the leg is bent or straight, i.e., that line runs through from the head to the hip-joint, middle of the knee, ankle and centre of his foot and toes.

The girl must at all times understand the very slight changes of weight that have to be made to remain on balance and the boy, at all times, must help her to maintain that centre. If she deviates from the perpendicular at any time, he must correct this. During the first lessons it is recommended that he removes his hands so that she may realise how important his help can be, and how she must achieve this centring of balance for herself.

## HOLDS WITH TWO HANDS ON THE WAIST
These are the first to be taken with the boy standing behind the girl in 2nd position. Palms of his hands are placed firmly on the sides of the girl's waist, 1st finger and thumb encircling the waist with the thumb resting on the large spinal muscles. Elbows and wrists directed downwards. He stands NOT VERY TURNED-OUT.

The least tension in the boy's arms or hands will hinder the girl's movement and he must adjust his hands, and particularly his wrists, to any movement of the girl's working leg as it moves in its socket. The girl must always centre her own weight in any position, particularly *sur les pointes* and keep her pelvis as still as possible, especially during the first lessons, and use her spine correctly, stretched away from her hips, except of course in *arabesque*.

**Ex. 1:** This should be taken without any movement, boy's hands on the girl's waist and merely directed towards an understanding of the necessary synchronisation of breathing, using the system described in the Introduction.

**Ex. 2:** *Relevés* in 5th position
N.B. The Russian school uses quarter *plié* and only springs from the pads of the toes to the full *pointe*; thus their *relevé* is little more than a rise.

Practise these *relevés* in various timings. Start very slow, quicken, and later use uneven timing. The boy must 'feel' the girl's weight if the *relevé* is to be held; see 'feeling and holding' in the Introduction, and sketch 2.

**Ex. 3:** *Relevé retiré.*

The boy must ensure that the girl's weight is centred over her supporting leg and exactly between his two feet before she moves into *fondu* or *demi-plié*. When she rises (or *relevé*) she must be helped to retain her centre and not incline her body, nor move her supporting foot; see sketches 3 and 4.

**Ex. 4:** *Relevés retirés* must also be practised from 2nd and 4th positions.

3. *Relevé* inclination from the perpendicular

4. *Demi-plié* and rise

**Ex. 5:** *Connecting and preparatory movements*

Both boy and girl must be able to control the length of the step to be taken, whether from a straight leg or *fondu*, and control that length at all times so that both travel the necessary distance.

The best way to understand the length of the step to be taken is to stand in 5th, transfer weight to the supporting leg and, holding it firmly in place, stretch the working leg outwards from the hip only. When it has reached its fullest extent drop the heel; the toe will come back a little. This gives the natural length of a step. A larger step is taken from *fondu*, the weight being retained firmly over the supporting leg until the working heel has reached the floor.

The size of the step to be taken is also determined by the depth of the *demi-plié* or *fondu*. If the working leg is to be raised no higher than 45°, then the *demi-plié* or *fondu* will be much smaller than if the leg is to be raised to 90°. This is particularly important if the girl has to *fondu sur les pointes* as a preparation for a *pirouette* or *tour* (see p 30). When stretching from a *fondu* into any type of movement it is desirable that both the supporting and the working leg are seen to stretch equally so that the true line of the movement is preserved.

The girl must always remember that the working toe (i.e., that moving into the step) must reach the floor before she transfers her weight. But more important, the moment the toe does reach the floor her weight is simultaneously transferred as the heel reaches the floor. If she does not make this immediate transfer, her centre of balance will not be directly over the new supporting leg. Similarly, if she has to make a preparation for a *pirouette*, e.g., *en dedans* from 4th, she must bend the front leg only and lower the back heel to the floor keeping that leg straight. In this way her weight remains centred over the supporting leg; see sketch 19.

The connecting and preparatory movements to be practised are *pas marchés*, *pas de bourrées* (with and without changing feet), *en tournant*, *pas couru*, *chassé*, etc. They must be practised with the boy behind the girl, two hands on her waist. He must concentrate on maintaining her centre of balance and controlling her weight in order to co-ordinate their movements.

**a.** In *pas de bourrées*, the boy should transfer the weight of the girl's body from one hand to the other when she repeats the movement to the opposite side; at the moment of change he should transfer his own weight from one leg to the other. He does NOT hold her, he only FEELS the movement.

**b.** In *pas de bourrées* with a change of feet and *épaulement*, the boy must help the girl and guide her body. N.B. This first introduces how to give impetus; see p 20.

**c.** In *pas de bourrées en tournant*, etc., the boy must give a slight impetus to the turn by lightly pressing his hand forwards on the side of the body coming into the turn, e.g., *en dedans* starting 4th, right foot *devant*. His left hand is on her left side and moves slightly forwards; the right moves backwards.

**d.** In *pas couru*, the boy should move simultaneously with the girl with simple walking steps or a repeated *chassé* in strict tempo.

**e.** In *pas balancé* and *glissades* the couple can move together, or if the girl dances round the boy, he can either turn with her or keep still. In the first case he must always hold her. In the second he must grasp her firmly as she finishes in some pose.

These steps should also be practised as movements towards the partner. The boy can stand in place, the girl moving towards him, carefully judging the correct distance so that he may grasp her easily, weight correctly centred. HE MUST NEVER MOVE, SHE MUST DO ALL THE WORK. However, if they both move towards each other, both must know how to space their steps and arrive at the centre together; see p 20.

Later, if the *glissade* is a preparation for a jump, the boy should hold one side of the girl's waist and move with her so that at the moment of jump he is very slightly behind and on one side of her and can guide her with the slight impetus he gives from that hand as he grasps her waist with the other hand.

**Ex. 6.** *Développé, grand ronds de jambe, passé, grand ports de bras—* see sketch 5.

During the first stages of training, the height of the girl's raised leg must be strictly controlled at either 45° or 90°. Only by controlling

5. *Develeloppé devant* at 90°
   inclination from the perpendicular

the height will she gain strength in the spinal muscles to keep her weight centred. And only if she controls the height of her leg will the boy learn to 'feel' the necessary adjustments to be made as her leg moves from position to position, particularly in *grand ronds de jambe* and *grand ports de bras*.

In *développés* at 45° or 90° the boy must keep the weight of the girl's body over her supporting leg and not allow it to sink or her working leg to twist. He must anticipate the feel of her weight coming slightly towards him as she lifts her leg, and before she lowers her heels, so that it is replaced over her two feet.

For example, the girl is in 5th *de face*, right *devant*. The boy is behind her, hands on her waist, as both make a slight *demi-plié*. She moves into *relevé* holding 5th, then *développé devant*. Whilst she is still in 5th on both feet, the boy slightly moves the weight of her body on to her left *pointe* and towards himself. When she feels she is on her left *pointe*, she begins the *développé*. The boy firmly holds her weight until the end of her movement, and when she lowers her leg to 5th *sur les pointes*, he transfers her weight slightly forwards on to her own feet. Both should finish in a slight *demi-plié* as she lowers her heels.

N.B. This serves as a preparation for another movement after finishing a jump at a later stage in training.

*Grand ports de bras sur les pointes* must be practised in all *pas de deux* with the help of the partner.

**Ex. 7:** The girl stands in 1st *arabesque* on right *pointe*; the boy is behind on right foot, left *pointe tendue derrière* (not too turned-out).

See sketch 6, and note that the leg is stretched *derrière* but resting on the ball of the foot, a position which acts as a better stabilising factor in most supported adage at any stage of training than any *pointe tendue*. The girl does *grand ports de bras devant* and into 2nd *arabesque* whilst the boy lightly but firmly helps her to transfer the weight of her body forwards by drawing his right hand slightly backwards and his left hand forwards with a tiny circular movement. HIS HANDS MUST BE KEPT EQUIDISTANT. When she returns to 1st *arabesque*, he reverses the movement of his hands.

N.B. *Grand ports de bras*, as in the usual classical class, can be taken at two levels: firstly where the girl bends or circles her body

13

6. The four *arabesques;* note position of boy's hands and his stance

roughly at or just under shoulder level, and secondly where she bends or circles her body from the waist. In Ex. 6, she must bend directly forwards from the waist-line as she moves her arms into preparatory position and recover her true *arabesque* line as she stretches her arms and body upwards again.

This exercise should also be practised using 3rd and 4th *arabesques* when the boy's hands must exercise greater control and his body also will turn a little from the waist upwards as she moves.

**Ex. 8:** *Small and large poses.*

These should be studied firstly by taking them from positions *en place*, and then with various steps into a pose. These latter exercises should be a combination of the boy standing *en place* and the girl taking one step towards him; later both taking one step towards each other, and finally the boy moving to the girl.

All the above should be practised (1) with the boy behind the girl; (2) standing side by side; (3) facing each other.

These poses are first studied with both the boy's hands on the girl's waist; then holding one hand only.

The movement towards the partner can be made with and without a hold. It is very important in the latter case that the boy anticipates

14

the moment when he must control the girl to centre her weight.

If the boy stands *en place* the girl must concentrate on the size of the step she takes towards him and move straight into a pose, leg or legs absolutely controlled and spine firmly held. This is even more important when both partners move towards each other.

The boy's pose or position must harmonise with that of the girl and he must always remember not to use full turn-out and also keep his own weight firmly fixed over the three points of balance of his foot or feet.

*Temps lié* at 90° is the most useful exercise for practice during the first lessons as it uses steps from *demi-plié* to pose, and *vice versa*; see sketches 7, 8 and 9.

7. *Attitude croisée* and *éffacée* with two hands hold

8. *Pose écarté devant* and *derrière* with two hands hold

9. *Pose croisée devant* and *éffacée* with two hands hold

## TURNS: DEFINITIONS
In the Russian school there are four kinds of turns:
1. *Turn* means the boy turns the girl without giving impetus.
2. *Promenade* means the boy turns the girl by walking round her.
3. *Revolve* means the boy and girl turn round each other forwards, backwards or *dos-à-dos*.
4. *Pirouettes* means the girl takes 'force' as in solo work and her partner holding his hands still in the appropriate position, away from but encircling her waist. Later on he must study how to give 'impetus' to increase the number of her revolves.

### Turns
Turns must be practised in various forms; the girl moving on one or both feet *sur le pointes*, the boy *en place* and turning her.

First attempts must be made slowly, the boy concentrating to maintain the girl's central line of balance. The first exercise should be based on *battement soutenu* (or *assemblé soutenu*). The boy stands behind the girl, who is *sur les pointes*, and makes a quarter, half, three-quarter and finally one full turn. He must learn to use his hands carefully, giving equal pressure on each side of her waist whilst directing one hand forwards and the other backwards. In such turns, HE ALWAYS PRESSES FORWARDS ON THE SIDE OF THE WAIST MOVING INTO THE TURN. THE GIRL MUST NOT RISE FROM HER *DEMI-PLIE* OR *FONDU* UNTIL SHE FEELS HIS HANDS CONTROLLING HER MOVEMENT.

If she does not use a *demi-plié* or *fondu* into a *relevé*, SHE MUST WAIT UNTIL THE BOY BEGINS TO GIVE IMPETUS; see sketch 10.

The boy must learn to control the movement of his hands so that the girl's turn is always smooth.

The next turns to be practised should finish with the boy taking a step or lunge to the side, depending on the girl's pose.

10. Preparatory position before *pirouette en dedans*

**Ex. 1:** see sketch 11.

The girl stands on left *pointe*, right *à la seconde* at 90°; the boy is behind with both hands on her waist. He firmly presses his right hand slightly forwards and the left backwards, and slowly turns her to her left. As she brings her leg into *retiré* she raises her arms to 3rd

11. Turn from *à la seconde* at 90 into *attitude croisée*

and finishes the turn in *attitude croisée*. At this moment the boy steps slightly or lunges forwards on his right foot.

### Other Aspects of Turns

There are other aspects of turns when the boy must change the line of his hands on the girl's waist to give impetus to her turn, e.g., in *grands fouettés*, *fouettés en tournant*, etc.

**Ex. 2:** see sketch 12.

The girl faces the boy on right *pointe*, left leg *à la seconde* at 90°, arms in 2nd. The boy is behind her and moves his right hand backwards and left forwards, slightly pressing her waist as she moves into an *en dedans* turn. During this the girl raises her arms to 3rd; her working leg is held at 90° during the turn into *attitude croisée*. She must hold the pose as the boy steps or lunges to the side or slightly forwards.

12. *A la seconde* at 90° facing the partner

### Promenades

*Promenades* are those movements when the girl stands *sur la pointe* in some pose and the boy, holding her waist or some part of her arm or body, walks round turning her *en place*. In her turn the girl must gradually pivot her supporting *pointe en place*.

In all *promenades* in small or large poses the boy, when using both hands on the girl's waist, must circle round her central point of balance, which is the toe of her supporting leg. Before turning to the right he should take his first step with the left foot, and his right foot as it moves keeps close to the left heel. It must not cross in front. When moving to the left, he commences with his right foot. Steps made in such a circle must be very smooth with little bend of the knees. This type of walk is used only when the boy is holding the girl's waist with both hands and making a circle close to and round her supporting leg.

All *promenades* must first be studied very slowly and the girl's position must never change. The boy must learn to use simple walking steps in a circle an arm's length away from the girl's central line of balance (see sketch 47) or side by side (e.g., using cradle hold or cross hands) or facing her. The boy must also move simultaneously with the girl, keeping his own centre of balance in line with the girl's so that her weight is always correctly maintained over her supporting leg.

## Pirouettes or tours

*Pirouettes* or *tours* in this section refer principally to those turns when the girl takes 'force' for a single or multiple series of turns on one *pointe*. All *pirouettes* are first practised with a single turn only, so that the boy learns to feel the girl taking 'force', and also judge the tempo (speed) of her turns as this can vary considerably.

Before studying *pirouettes* in double-work it is essential to restate the general rules and practice of the correct preparations.

Girls must know that, when turning with a partner, the same rules apply as in solo dance, the only difference being that the boy can help increase the number of turns at a later stage in training.

During these early stages both the boy and girl must get to know the tempo at which the particular partner turns, and must practise various ways of timing the preparation so the movements coincide.

In such exercises, i.e., without turning, the boy must fully understand the various changes to be made in the girl's centre line of balance as she rises from a *demi-plié* or *fondu* and after she finishes the turn. The girl's equilibrium must be maintained from the moment she takes 'force' to move into the turn. The teacher must insist that the girl's poise is always correct and adheres to the classical lines.

Without studying the rise from the preparation, the boy cannot help the girl during the *pirouette*, nor increase the number of her turns.

**Ex. 3:** see sketch 13.

The preparation before a single *pirouette en dehors* from 4th position. The girl stands in 5th, right foot *devant*, arms in preparatory position. The boy stands behind her in 2nd or 4th opposite 1st, both hands on her waist. She moves into *demi-plié* and *relevé* on left foot, bringing the right *sur le cou de pied devant* and arms to 1st. At this moment the boy transfers the weight of the girl's body very slightly forwards as he moves his right foot backwards. Only after this

13. Preparation for *pirouettes* from 4th position and during the turn

should the girl take a correct 4th with right arm in 1st, left in 2nd, palm facing the floor. She then moves into a single *pirouette* with *relevé* on left, right foot *sur le cou de pied devant*, immediately bringing her left arm into 1st. The boy again slightly changes the girl's centre of balance from two feet to one foot, and draws his own right foot forwards again to stand erect.

This type of preliminary *pirouette* should be practised ending in small and large poses.

Preparation before *pirouettes* from 4th or 5th *en dehors* or *en dedans* are first studied *de face* in very slow tempo; but later it is very important to add *épaulement* facing points 2 or 8.

Before studying any *pirouette* with a partner the girl must use her arms according to the following rules:
1. If going into 1st, one arm must quickly join the other already curved across the chest, thus using a shortened 1st; see sketch 14. It is very important that the girl's elbows are held away from the sides of her body so that the boy's hands are not in any way impeded. Ideally, the height of the girl's hands is at the level of her breast-bone, from 4-5 inches away.

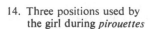

14. Three positions used by
    the girl during *pirouettes*

19

2. If going into 3rd, both arms must be raised from 2nd directly above the head, the one from 2nd, the other from 1st without any deviation forwards or backwards so that the weight of the body does not move from the central line of balance and is directly over the supporting leg. The elbows and wrists must be held firmly with shoulders and hips level in order not to disturb the boy's stance.

The basic problems facing the boy in all *pirouettes* during double-work are the following:

1. During the girl's walk or step and/or preparation for *pirouettes* the boy must feel that her weight is correctly centered at all times and help her to find the most comfortable position in which to take 'force' for the *pirouette*.
2. During the *pirouette* the boy must keep the girl's weight firmly centered over her supporting leg and if she deviates from the perpendicular, must correct her firmly to restore her equilibrium.
3. The boy must always co-ordinate and harmonise his own position and stance with the classical line made by the girl.

For stage work the girl's working foot should be raised from the *sur le cou de pied*, which is first practised, to a point where the tips of her toes reach the centre of the calf. However, modern choreographers and ballerinas often hold the working leg as high as the knee, or even higher. This is not recommended for beginners.

At the beginning of training the girl should not turn more than a single *pirouette*, thus allowing the boy to 'feel' how he can help her turn. In later classes however, when the girl must do multiple turns, the boy must help during the preparatory *demi-plié* and slightly change the line of his hands on her waist in a contrary direction to the way in which she will turn. At the moment when she takes 'force' he must simultaneously reverse the slight movement of his hands to give her extra impetus. During this slight push-pull movement, his hands must be kept level and equidistant.

The difference between the girl taking 'force' and the boy giving 'impetus' is most important. The use of these two terms is not identical. To take 'force' in the Russian school is to bring 'force' behind the shoulder coming into the *pirouette* whether the dancer is boy or girl, and is working as an individual. To give 'impetus' is to make a strong movement on one or another part of the partner's body to propel it into a particular direction, e.g., the strong push of the boy's hand to propel the girl into a high *assemblé* which he makes on her waist. The word 'impetus' is therefore used for that subtle and extra pull-push movement in double-work by the boy, particularly in *pirouettes*, which gives the girl something extra as she moves into her *pirouette*.

If the girl deviates from the perpendicular in any *pirouette* then the boy must lightly but firmly restore her to the correct position by a strong and controlled pressure from his hands—but NOT FROM HIS FINGERS. Whether the *pirouettes* are slow or fast, they must be smooth and clean, the girl making full use of her head. There are however cases, not usually in classical dance, where the partners do depart from these rules.

If the girl is turning multiple *pirouettes*, the boy must keep his elbows well down and guide her body within the circle between his thumb and forefinger, the other fingers and palm flat on the girl's waist once he has helped to give 'impetus' as she rises from the preparation into the turn; see sketch 15.

When the girl is taking multiple *pirouettes* on the stage, it is usual for one of the boy's hands to follow – as it were – her turn by helping her to revolve with a lightly repeated pressure from that hand. This is a very subtle movement, for any such help must never be obvious to the audience.

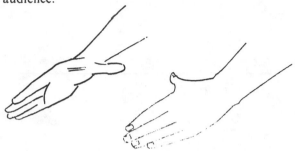

15. Position of the boy's hands on the girl's waist during *pirouettes*

Every girl takes 'force' for *pirouettes* in her own individual way. For example: some use a short, sharp *demi-plié* to take 'force'; others a soft *plié* and slow movement of the arm. Some may incline from the perpendicular when taking 'force' as they *relevé*, or during the turn and shift forwards, backwards or to the right, left, etc. The boy must therefore be fully aware of his responsibilities and feel these slight nuances in her change of weight throughout the turn and if possible anticipate them in order to help the girl achieve the maximum amount of turns without loss of equilibrium.

The number and beauty of the *pirouettes* used in double-work depends not only on the technical accomplishment of the danseuse, but also on the danseur's dexterity and co-ordination as he 'feels' the tempo and quality of her movements.

### *Pirouettes* from 4th position
After *demi-plié* in 4th, the girl takes 'force' as she does in solo dance. During the *pirouettes* the boy's hands frame the girl's waist, slightly propelling her onwards as he gently works his hands. During the *pirouettes* the boy controls the girl's waist with the palms of both hands and NOT the fingers. All *pirouettes* from 4th must be practised finishing in small and large poses.

### *Pirouettes* from 5th position
Preparations for *pirouettes* from 5th are usually taken with a *relevé retiré* to the level of *sur le cou de pied devant* or *derrière*. Only when this is mastered should the working foot be raised to mid-calf. The *pirouettes* must then be studied *en dehors* and *en dedans* ending in small and large poses.

21

*Pirouettes en dehors* from *croisé*–sketch 16

An example: the girl stands in *attitude croisée devant* on right *pointe* at 45°, her right arm in 1st and left in 2nd. The boy stands in 2nd behind her, both hands on her waist. He then changes his hands slightly along the same line, right forwards and left slightly backwards, and reverses the movement as he firmly presses both hands to give 'impetus' to the turn. Simultaneously the girl takes 'force' and *pirouettes en dehors*. During the turn the boy keeps his hands round her waist and follows the general rules for *pirouettes* given earlier.

16. Preparatory position before a
    turn

During practice it is useful to take *pirouettes* from a *croisé* position at the same time as *pirouettes* from 4th. Those from 4th should often finish *à la seconde* at 90° and this can be followed by *passé* into another pose *croisé* and another *pirouette etc:*.

*Pirouettes* from 1st *arabesque*–sketch 17

The girl stands in 1st *arabesque* on left *pointe*. The boy, standing behind her, left *fondu* and right *pointe tendue*, places both hands on her waist. He then slightly changes his hands along the line of her waist, pressing the left backwards and the right forwards and slightly upwards, thus giving 'impetus' to the turn as he helps the girl to return to the perpendicular, her weight correctly centred. At this moment the girl takes 'force' into a *pirouette en dedans* by whipping her working leg directly into *retiré devant* and raising her arms to 3rd position.

These same principles are used when studying *pirouettes* from 3rd *arabesque*, boy standing behind the girl: and from 4th *arabesque*, both working face to face; from *pose écarté*, e.g., the girl left *écarté* to point 8, the boy standing facing her.

17. *Pirouettes en dedans*
    from 1st *arabesque*

All the above poses are taken as a preparation before the girl's *pirouette*, and must be studied both *en dehors* and *en dedans*, the girl preparing with and without *demi-plié* before taking 'force'.

*Pirouettes* from a step, *tombé* or *preparation dégagé*–see p 20
*Pas de deux* can combine several types of turns and *pirouettes*, the girl starting the preparation or even moving into the turn itself before the boy approaches her during the turn or *pirouette*.

**Ex. 1:** The girl faces point 7 in 2nd *arabesque à terre* on left foot. The boy stands about two steps behind her on same foot. She then turns towards him taking one step on right foot and into *posé* left foot, raising arms to 3rd and turning a *pirouette en dehors*. The boy brings his right arm forwards, elbow down, palm sideways and, 'feeling' the side of the girl's waist, guides her into the perpendicular position. He then places the palm of his left hand firmly on her waist in the usual position; see sketch 18.

**Ex. 2:** The girl does several *tours enchaînés* in a diagonal line from point 6-2, coming no nearer than two steps away from the boy where she falls (*tombé*) on to her right foot and immediately steps on left *pointe* for a *pirouette en dehors* – at least 2 turns. The boy takes hold of her waist as in Ex. 1.

**Ex. 3:** After a given amount of *tours enchaînés* the girl, with *fondu* on left and *relevé* on right does *pirouette en dedans*. The boy takes hold as above.

18. Preparation before a step into a
   *pirouette*

*Tours* or *pirouettes à la seconde* at 90° from 4th–sketch 19
The girl stands 4th *croisé*, right *fondu devant*, right arm in 1st, left in 2nd. The boy stands in 1st at her side in such a position that she cannot touch him during her *pirouette*. The girl then does a single *pirouette à la seconde* at 90° (as in solo work). When her working leg has just passed him, the boy takes a large step towards her, places his two hands on her waist, and holds her firmly in the final pose.

19. Preparatory position before a *pirouette* from 4th into *à la seconde* at 90°

The final pose in all the above *pirouettes* or turns should be practised in *attitude croisée*, 3rd *arabesque* and other poses common to classical ballet. They should also be practised with preparations with and without *demi-plié* (i.e., from a *relevé*, *pas de bourrée*) and straight from some pose.

## FALLING POSES AND POSITIONS USING TWO HANDS

The girl stands in 5th *sur les pointes*, right foot *croisé devant*, arms in 3rd, and her body turned slightly upwards and to the right. The boy is behind her, arms round her waist, his left hand clasping his right wrist; see sketch 20. He places his left foot beside her *pointes*, and so bends his right arm as he lunges sideways on his left foot, as the girl rests in the crook of his right arm. To return the girl to her original position, he must strongly stretch his right leg and bring it back to

20. Lowering the girl into a 'falling' position

his left, in the original starting position. He must not change the position of his hands during the 'fall'. The girl also must not deviate in any way from her original stance.

This exercise should also be practised, lowering the girl both with her spine and with her face to the floor. In the former case she must keep her spine absolutely straight. In the latter case she must slightly arch her back and curve her head, but hold her pose very firmly throughout the 'fall'; see sketch 21.

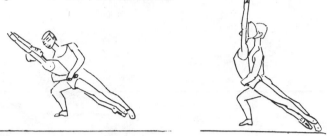

21. Lowering the girl into a 'falling' position with her spine or her face to the floor

## HAND HOLDS

In all classical *pas de deux* the girl's arms must be used as they are in solo work, the only difference being that, when the partners take hands, the palms of their hands can face upwards or downwards and adapt themselves to the needs of the particular exercise. The boy must hold the girl either over or under her hand, palm to palm or by the wrist. If he holds her from above, the palms of his hands lie over hers, the tips of his fingers resting just under her hand. This is the simplest and safest hold in the following examples, particularly when the girl is using 2nd position; see sketch 22. The hand must also be so held that the partners' hands are in full contact, his fingers always protecting hers; see sketch 23.

During all such movements the boy's hands must not press downwards on the girl's arms but must be kept level; see sketch 24.

There are of course other holds which come into use at a later stage, e.g., the boy takes the girl by one arm, the other on her waist, or she holds her hands on the boy's arms, shoulders, etc.

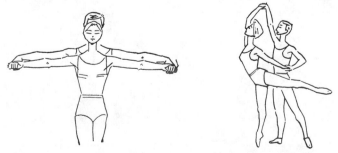

22. Holding the girl by her wrists or palm to palm

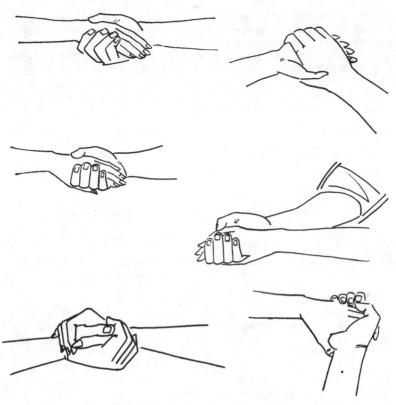

23. Various holds using palm to palm

24. Holding the girl by her wrists

**Turns**

During simple turns in 5th position and turns using *battement soutenu* (*assemblé*) *sur les pointes,* the boy gives strength to the turn with one or both hands so that the girl can make a quarter, half or full turn. After this the boy can again take both her hands or replace his own on her waist.

It is also useful to use the same rules if the girl is turning with *pas de bourrée* or *flic-flac en tournant.*

*Basic full turn, the boy holding the girl with two hands*–sketch 25
The girl stands with her back to point 1 on her right *pointe,* left *sur le cou de pied derrière,* right arm in 3rd, left in 1st position, palm downwards. The boy faces her, her right hand in his and her left in his, (i.e., both in 1st position). The turn begins from this position, the arms moving through three positions:

1. The boy opens his left arm to the side, turning the girl until her spine faces him. Their right arms are still in 3rd, thus stabilizing the girl's vertical position.
2. The boy now opens their right arms to the side and then lifts their left arms to 3rd.
3. The boy returns their right arms to 1st position.

During the turn the girl helps by gradually pivoting on her supporting leg in the direction of the turn and maintaining her centre of balance over her supporting *pointe.*

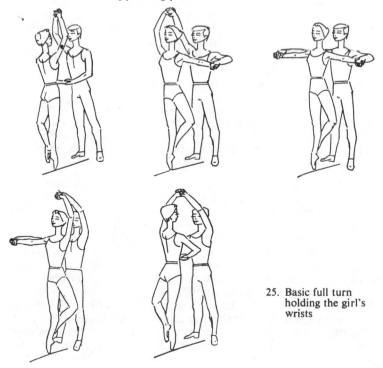

25. Basic full turn
holding the girl's
wrists

This turn must be practised to the other side. Whether the girl turns on her right or left *pointe*, the movement must always be practised very slowly with careful attention to detail. Only when both partners never deviate from the perpendicular position can the movement be quickened, for then they will be at complete ease with each other.

## Other aspects of turns

Before the movement begins for a half turn *à la seconde* at 90° and *grand fouetté en tournant*, the boy holds the girl's two hands in his and gives strength to the turn, which she then accomplishes on her own by pushing away from his hands. He can only stabilize her balance by placing them back again on her waist as she finishes in the appropriate pose.

If the boy takes her arms again he must do this at the very moment when she finishes. To perform this he must stand behind or facing her, holding her hands from above and palm to palm, or by her wrists or elbows. In this case he stands behind her and holds her elbows from underneath, just a little nearer the elbow joints.

When taking *grand fouetté* from an *éffacée* position from both hands, the boy must seem to urge the girl's hands onwards but without spoiling the curved line they are making.

## Promenades

During *promenades* using both hands, the boy simply walks round the girl in part of or a whole circle, the axis of which is the girl's supporting leg. If the turn is to the left then his first step is made with the right foot; if to the right then he begins with his left foot.

In those cases when the boy leads the girl backwards in the circle, he usually begins in the same way. But in those cases when the turn is to the right, it is far better to begin with the right foot, and if to the left then with the left foot.

The girl always uses her supporting *pointe* as she does in all turns performed as mentioned earlier, with both hands on the waist.

All such *promenades* must first be practised slowly and without any change of pose; later the tempo must be quickened and a change of pose take place during the *promenade*.

**Ex. 1:** *Promenade en attitude* during which the girl holds both hands on the boy's arms – see sketch 26.

The boy stands in 4th, right foot *éffacée devant*, weight firmly centred over his right leg, left stretched backwards on the ball of the foot. His right arm is stretched forwards, his left in 2nd, palm upwards, head turned to the left. The girl takes *attitude éffacée* on right *pointe*, placing her left hand on the boy's left and her right on his right shoulder. Once the girl has stabilised her balance, the boy straightens his right leg and, commencing right foot, slowly circles to the left.

Before such a *promenade* the girl usually begins with a *glissade, pas couru* or simple step towards the boy. She must calculate her preparation so that she does not pass him, nor press or lower her own arms during the circling. This *promenade* should be studied using other poses.

**Ex. 2:** *Promenade en attitude*, the boy holding the girl by cradling one arm round her waist, the other holding her hand – see sketch 27.

The girl stands in *attitude de face* on left *pointe*; the boy is on her left. He cradles his right arm round the back of her body so that the tips of his fingers rest on the front of her left hip. He holds her left hand in his left. The boy circles to the right; during the *promenade* he must not straighten his left elbow. He must be close to the girl, controlling the line of her hips and never allowing her to lose her balance nor to deviate from the close circle he is making. At the same time it must be seen that there is 'air' and 'light' between the partners, even if the girl is wearing a long and very full skirt, as in *Les Sylphides*.

26. *Promenade* in *attitude*, girl holding boy's shoulder and arm

27. *Promenade* in *attitude*, boy using cradle hold round girl's waist

This *promenade* must be studied in all the *grands* and *petits poses* and from varied preparations. One of the most interesting is that shown in sketch 28. The boy holds the girl's left hand in his left and his right cradled round her body and holding her left hip.

**Ex. 3:** The partners face each other and *promenade à la seconde* at 90°, holding both hands – see sketch 29.

The girl stands with her back to point 1 in 5th *sur les pointes*, right foot *devant*, arms in 3rd. The boy faces her, arms in 2nd, palms upwards. The girl opens her arms to 2nd and places her hands on his

28. *Promenade* in *attitude*, boy's hand on girl's hip

29. *Promenade à la seconde* at 90°, using palm to palm hold

as she does *développé à la seconde* at 90° with right leg. Before commencing the *promenade* the boy must slightly turn his hips to the left, i.e., the line his circle will take, but keep his shoulders facing the girl. During the *promenade* both boy and girl must hold their arms firmly in 2nd and maintain the space between them.

## Pirouettes

**Ex. 1:** *Pirouettes* from *à la seconde* at 90° holding hands.

These *pirouettes* should be studied from a stabilized position *à la seconde* at 90° going straight into the turn without any stop after the *promenade*, both *en dehors* and *en dedans*, with and without a *fondu* before the turn. The preparation is taken immediately after the *promenade*. The girl takes 'force' by pressing away from the boy's hands and raising her arms to 3rd. At this moment the boy lightly but firmly guides the girl's arms upwards and then places both hands on her waist as she completes her *pirouette*.

**Ex. 2:** *Pirouettes à la seconde* at 90° holding the girl's wrists.
This can be studied in two ways, either the boy stands behind the girl; or he can face her.

The girl faces point 1 on left *pointe à la seconde* at 90°. The boy is behind her holding her wrists in both hands, palms upwards. Giving her right leg an extra stretch to the side away from the turn, the girl pushes away from the boy's hands to take 'force' and turns *en dehors*. Her right leg must not deviate from *à la seconde*. During the turn she can keep her arms in 2nd or raise them to 3rd. After the boy has helped her to take 'force', he must take a large step backwards and, only when her leg has passed him, can he swiftly return ready to take her two hands or place his own round her waist. If the boy faces the girl it is more usual to turn *en dedans*, but using the same technique.

**Ex. 3:** *Pirouette en dehors* from *pose croisé devant* – sketch 30.

The girl stands facing point 8 on left *pointe*, right *sur le cou de pied devant*, right arm in 3rd, left in 2nd. The boy behind her raises his right hand palm upwards and takes her right in his right, his left in her left. Before taking 'force' the girl slightly presses her right leg against the turn and simultaneously the boy lowers her right arm into 2nd. She can then use the strength of both his arms to move into

30. Preparatory position before *pirouette en dedans* from pose *croisè devant*

the turn. The girl immediately draws her arms into 1st and the boy is then able to place his hands on her waist.

After the *pirouette* the boy holds the girl in *attitude croisée* or some suitable pose. When the girl takes 'force', i.e., immediately before she turns, it is very important for him to judge the correct tempo, as so much depends upon the partners exactly co-ordinating their movements, and deciding upon the quality and quantity of turns to be made.

When first studying these *pirouettes* the boy must NEVER use his arms to give 'force'. He can only give strength so that the girl pushes away from his hands. He can guide her hands accurately to 3rd if she raises them before he places his own hands on her waist. These *pirouettes* should be studied both *en dehors* and *en dedans*.

**Ex. 4:** *Pirouettes en dedans* from *attitude*, the girl placing both hands on the boy's arms.

In studying this type of turn, the theory of *pirouettes* must be fully understood. The preparation must be practised and mastered before any *pirouette* is undertaken.

The girl is in *attitude éffacée* on right *pointe*, her left hand rests on the boy's left hand, her right on his shoulder; see sketch 26. She brings her left foot swiftly *sur le cou de pied devant* and her arms to 3rd. After taking 'force' the girl falls into the boy's arms as he lunges backwards and stops her by placing both arms round her waist. The timing of this 'fall' must be very accurate. Once this *pirouette* and fall have been mastered, it must be practised using other poses.

**Ex. 5:** *Pirouette* from 1st *arabesque*, holding the girl's wrists – see sketch 31.

These turns are usually practised *en dedans*. The boy stands behind the girl on his right foot, *arabesque à terre*, holding her wrists in both hands. He gives her strength to commence the turn with his left hand and raises her right arm to 3rd to help her recover the vertical position as she brings her left arm into 1st. During the *pirouette*, he holds her right wrist softly allowing her to turn easily, but at the same time maintains her weight over her supporting leg. If the girl wishes to finish her *pirouette* in 1st *arabesque*, the boy must catch her by her left wrist as she finishes and return her right arm to its original position.

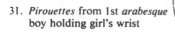

31. *Pirouettes* from 1st *arabesque* boy holding girl's wrist

From such a position the girl can also change arms as she turns. In these cases the boy releases her right wrist, and immediately takes her left. This change of hands must take place when the girl's arms are in 3rd.

This turn can also be practised in a low *attitude*; the boy then moves a little away from the girl, but without disturbing her balance or displacing her raised arm.

**Ex. 6:** *Pirouette en dehors* from *pose croisé devant*, the girl holding the boy's middle finger – sketch 32.

The girl stands facing point 8 on her left *pointe*, right *sur le cou de pied devant*, her left arm in 2nd and her right in 3rd, encircling her partner's middle finger with her own. The boy is behind her, his right arm over her head, middle finger directed downwards. He takes the girl's left hand under his, palm to palm. She takes 'force' by moving her right foot against the turn, at the same time pushing away from the boy's left hand as he stabilises her position. During the *pirouette* she encircles the boy's finger with her own but NEVER FULLY STRAIGHTENS HER ARM. When she finishes, the boy takes her left hand and holds her in the original position.

The boy's left arm must be held strongly so that the girl can push against it. His right hand must be just over and slightly in front of the girl's head, and never slacken or move it in any way.

*Pirouettes* on the boy's finger can begin in many different ways but the principle is always the same.

**Ex. 7:** *Pirouettes en dedans* from 1st *arabesque* – sketch 33.

In these *pirouettes* there are two variations; the boy can be kneeling, the girl walking or running to him; or they can approach each other and then the boy kneels on one knee.

In the first example the boy is kneeling on his right knee facing point 7, arms in 2nd, palms upwards. The girl faces the boy, back to point 7 from three to four steps away. She walks or runs to him and

32. Position of boy's and girl's fingers for a *pirouette* on the index finger

33. *Pirouettes en dedans* from 1st *arabesque* on the boy's hands

places both hands on his as she moves into 1st *arabesque* on right *pointe*. She must calculate her approach so that when she finishes, he can place his hands on her waist. The girl then pushes away from his hands taking 'force' to *pirouette en dedans*. During the turn the boy places both hands on her waist whilst kneeling on one knee.

## SUPPORTED ADAGE USING 'FALLS' INTO POSES AND POSITIONS

**Exs 1 & 2:** Lowering the girl from 1st *arabesque* holding both wrists or hands – sketches 34 and 35.

The girl stands in 1st *arabesque* (high) on her right *pointe*. The boy is behind her holding her wrists in his hands. To steady the girl as he lowers her, he braces his left foot against her left toe and with a *fondu* on his left, stretches his right leg towards point 3 as he brings his left arm smoothly down and across his torso, slightly bending his left wrist upwards as he lowers the girl. His left arm will thus be the stabilising factor if the girl's descent into the final pose is not to fall out of line; see sketch 20.

To return the girl to 1st *arabesque* the boy must give a sharp but steady pull with both arms towards himself. He must take care to keep his left arm firm and still as he draws his right foot back to his left. In this example, the girl must begin by falling towards her right hip and not allow her legs to slacken in any way. The boy must also be conscious of re-centring his own as well as her weight as he pulls her back to 1st *arabesque*. She too must keep her legs fully stretched. This fall can also be performed with the partners' hands palm to palm; see sketch 35.

After the 'fall' the girl must always return to 1st *arabesque*. The boy can then let go her left hand as she closes in 5th *sur les pointes*. At a later stage, she can move into another pose or position, the boy placing his hands on her waist, or wherever appropriate to the following movement.

34. Lowering the girl into a 'falling' position holding her wrists

35. Lowering the girl into a 'falling' position holding the palms of her hands

33

**Ex. 3:** Lowering the girl from 1st *arabesque* holding both hands as the partners remain back to back – sketch 36.

The partners stand face to face one step apart, she with her back to point 7, he with his back to point 3. With one step forwards the girl does *posé*, left foot into *attitude croisée*, arms in 2nd. The boy takes both hands, palm to palm, i.e., common hold. He then lifts her left arm into 3rd as he draws her right arm into preparatory position. At this moment the girl brings her right leg into *tire-bouchon* or *sur le cou de pied* and he moves his own arm into 2nd, leaving his right arm in 3rd. As they both turn their backs to each other and the girl's bent leg is about to touch the boy, he places his left foot against her supporting leg and they smoothly rest back to back. The girl now stretches her right leg into *développé devant* at 90°. Maintaining the straight line running through from his head and body to his left leg, he smoothly lunges to point 3 on his right foot, lowering the girl as she rests straight down his back. At the moment of 'falling' the girl must in no way slacken the straight and fully stretched line running through her body from the crown of her head to the supporting toe. With the help of the right foot only, the boy can now return to his upright position and thus replace the girl over her own centre of balance.

36. Lowering the girl into a 'falling' position from *attitude* holding her hands

There are many variations to add to this form of 'fall' after the partners have returned to the upright position. For example, the girl can bring her right foot through 1st position and move into 1st *arabesque*, the boy releasing her hands quickly and turning towards her, placing his own on her waist and so on.

**Ex. 4:** Lowering the girl holding one hand on her waist, the other on her wrist – sketch 37.

*First variation.* The girl stands in 5th position, right foot *devant*, right arm in 3rd, and left in 2nd. The boy is behind her, holding her right wrist in his right hand, his left arm cradled round her body, tips of his fingers reaching as far as the inner edge of her right hip. His left foot is braced at the side of her left foot when she rises *sur les pointes*. He then turns the girl to face point 3 at the same time as he smoothly lunges towards point 3 on his right foot. Simultaneously, both boy

37. Lowering the girl into a
'falling' position, one hand
on her waist the other
holding her waist

and girl stretch their right arms forwards as he lowers her to the required pose.

As they make this movement, both boy and girl must 'feel' how the level of their shoulder girdle is firmly maintained because their bodies are in such close contact. In moving into and returning from this pose the boy's right arm plays just as an important part as his left. The girl must be returned to her original position as in the preceding exercise.

On other occasions, before the girl is lowered as above, she can prepare for the 'fall' by using poses into 1st *arabesque* or *attitude éffacée*; later the exercise should be practised without holding the girl's wrist.

*Second variation.* The girl stands in 5th position, right foot *devant*, arms in 3rd. The boy is behind her holding her left wrist in his left hand. Placing his left foot by the girl's *pointes*, he places his right arm round her body so that his fingers reach her left hip. He turns the girl towards point 3 and lunges in the same direction on his right foot, his left hand still holding her left wrist, i.e., the girl is in the same position as above, but the boy's arms are differently placed.

*Third variation.* The girl is in 1st *arabesque* on her right foot. The boy stands behind her holding her wrists in both hands. He releases her left hand as she brings her foot into 5th *devant* and her left arm into 3rd, making a half turn so that she is back to point 3. He firmly places his left arm round her waist and, bracing his left foot against her *pointes*, lunges towards point 3 thus lowering the girl backwards.

The principle of releasing the girl's hand and turning her in a vertical position is the same as that used in all other 'falling' exercises.

## HOLDS WITH ONE HAND

All the movements studied earlier using two hands on the waist must now be repeated using one hand only. The most usual examples to practice are: holding one hand or wrist, or placing it on the body and encircling the body in some way.

For example; the girl stands in *attitude éffacée* on her left *pointe*. The boy is to her left, his right arm embracing her body. She bends her left arm at the elbow and wrist and places them on his right

35

ioulder. As she moves from this position into *développé passé* into a *grand rond de jambe* and other movements, the boy must always remember that her body will incline to the side away from the working leg. Therefore he must be on the alert and help her to control her body and guide it in the necessary direction. In all such situations, the girl must control the movement of her arms very strictly.

**Ex. 1:** See sketch 38.

The girl stands in 5th *éffacée*, right foot *devant*. Thence she kneels on her left knee and sinks to the floor, stretching her right leg to point 2, right arm in 1st, left in 2nd, palms down. Her left shoulder is tilted slightly downwards and her back slightly inclined away from her right leg. The boy stands facing her and lunges forwards on his left foot in a diagonal from point 2–6. The position of his arms is at the discretion of the teacher. He then offers his right hand to the girl who takes it with a flowing upwards gesture and places her right hand in his right. He firmly clasps it and, giving a signal for the movement to begin, helps the girl to rise from the floor. She first stretches upwards from her left knee, then steps on to the right *pointe* in *attitude éffacée* or 1st *arabesque*; see sketch 39.

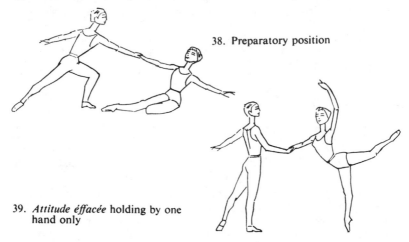

38. Preparatory position

39. *Attitude éffacée* holding by one hand only

During the entire movement, the girl must not bend her right arm nor pull on her partner's arm until she reaches *attitude*. When the boy gives the signal, he draws his left foot backwards, helping the girl to recover the upright position and re-centre her weight correctly *sur les pointes*. The boy must not pull the girl's arm away from its shoulder socket. She must help by holding her own shoulder down firmly.

When arranging student adage and allegro in double-work, the teacher should vary his exercises as much as possible, creating new situations which offer further problems, sometimes making them complicated in order to develop the students' dexterity and feeling for control over movement, as well as quickening their responses to the need always to obtain and maintain equilibrium, no matter what difficulties may present themselves.

**Turns with one hand**

The girl must understand that turns with one hand are her responsibility, her supporting foot actively helping the turn so that the boy's hand scarcely moves, although it is a stabilising factor. The boy only gives strength to the turn by helping her to keep her weight centred, so that if she wishes to retain the pose or make a change during the turn, his hand acts as the guide and focus of her axis.

**Ex. 1:** The girl stands with her back to point 1 on her right *pointe*, left *sur le cou de pied*, right arm in 3rd, palm turned towards the boy, left in preparatory position. The boy, facing the girl, offers his right hand and takes her right in his, palm to palm. His left arm is open in 2nd. From this position, the boy makes the necessary movement with his right hand and begins to turn the girl to the right, smoothly but firmly. During the turn, the girl's right arm is kept in 3rd position, over and just in front of the crown of her head. The boy must not allow her, or his arm, to incline to the front, side or back.

After the partners have taken hands and the girl begins to turn, the following transition of hands must take place. From the original position the boy, with a gliding movement, turns his right wrist edgeways into the turn and over their joined palms. In this way the girl can smoothly slip her right hand round his, but must never push his hands away nor weaken her own arm.

**Ex. 2:** See sketch 25. Full turns have been dealt with in the paragraphs about holds with two hands (see p. 10). These turns must be practised the boy holding with one hand only.

The preparation is the same, but the boy holds his left arm in 1st position with palm upwards and the girl with palm down when they join hands. The boy then opens his right arm into 2nd, thus helping the girl to make a half turn so that she is back to him. At this moment he raises both their right arms to 3rd and makes a strong movement with his wrist, thus helping the girl to complete the turn. She must keep her right arm very firm as he lifts it to 3rd. This turn should be practised to both sides. The position of the clasped hands of boy and girl must remain steady, palm to palm and strongly held. The right (or left) arms alone change their level.

Turns on one hand are also used, the boy holding the girl by the wrist. This type of turn requires a strong, steady movement from the boy's wrist. The girl co-ordinates her turn with this movement by the exact but tiny turn as she pivots on her supporting *pointe* as mentioned earlier.

**Ex. 3:** A half or three-quarter turn, the boy holding the girl with one hand on the waist.

The girl stands in *attitude croisée* on her left *pointe*. The boy, standing by her left shoulder, holds his right hand over her body, round the waist from the right side as far as the centre of her waist. He turns her to the left and moves backwards, trying all the time to remain behind her left shoulder. She moves into 1st *arabesque*.

The boy could also hold the girl's right hip, bringing the upper side of his forearm downwards and slightly forwards as extra support; see sketch 42.

If one movement of the boy's hand cannot turn the girl into the correct pose, he makes a quick, steady movement with his arm along the line of her waist towards the side moving against the turn, i.e., to the left.

## Promenades

*Promenades* holding the girl must be studied in all the basic poses of classical dance during the early stages of training. The girl's hand holding the boy's can be in 1st, 2nd or 3rd positions. In every case, her arm must be held firmly still, that is, with a straight line running through the centre of the bones from shoulder to elbow and wrist no matter whether the arm is bent or straight, nor at what level. It must not move during the *promenade*.

**Ex. 1:** *Promenade* holding the girl with one hand, palm to palm.

The girl steps into *attitude éffacée* on right *pointe*. The boy, facing the girl, proffers his right hand, palm upwards. She places her right hand firmly on his, arm in 1st position (i.e. the joined hands must be opposite her breast-bone). In this position the boy *promenades* round her to the right. His steps must be smooth and musically rhythmic. Each step is part of the circle and must be equidistant from the girl's supporting leg. During the *promenade* she must hold her pose without moving.

At the beginning of training it is essential that any *promenade* is taken slowly and should be incorporated into different *enchâainements*.

**Ex. 2:** *Promenade* holding the girl's wrist – see sketch 40.

1. The girl stands in 1st *arabesque* (high) on her right *pointe*. The boy stands on his left foot, right foot *pointe tendue derrière*, and takes her right wrist in his right hand.

To achieve this *promenade*, the boy must maintain exactly the same stance as above whilst making a circle to the left. If, on the other hand, the boy holds the girl's left wrist, then he must circle to the right.

2. The girl stands *écarté devant* or *derrière* on her left *pointe*. The boy stands slightly behind and to her left on his left foot, right *pointe tendue à la seconde*, and holds her right wrist in his right hand. Her left arm is opened to 2nd, just in front and across the boy's chest; see sketch 41. As before during such a *promenade* in this position, the boy must move directly behind and round the girl's spine, to help her to maintain her weight directly over her own supporting leg. This is the most difficult of *promenades*, but conforms to all the principles stated earlier.

**Ex. 3:** *Promenade* holding the girl with one hand on her body – see sketch 42.

In this *promenade* the boy uses the same principles as stated above, in particular those studied earlier relating to *ports de bras* (see p. 13), but using one hand on her waist.

40. 1st *arabesque* (high) holding the girl's wrist

41. *Pose écarté* holding the girl's right wrist

42. 1st *arabesque* (low), the boy holding the girl's right thigh with his right hand

The girl stands in 1st *arabesque* on her left *pointe*. The boy places the palm of his right hand firmly on her right hip at waist level, and stands so that his left foot is directly in the same line as her supporting toe and waist. His right foot is *pointe tendue derrière*. From this position the girl performs *grand ports de bras devant*. As she begins to stretch downwards, the boy slightly, but calmly, directs her body forwards, taking care not to disturb her equilibrium. Her movement depends entirely on her own ability to tilt (bow) her pelvis over her supporting leg without arching her spine. He can only help her to maintain a perpendicular supporting leg.

During the *ports de bras*, the girl's pose should acquire elegance and lightness. She must retain the depth of this pose throughout the *promenade*, whilst the boy concentrates on keeping her weight centred over the supporting leg.

The girl should first master the technique of moving into the low *arabesque* using this particular hold, and only when that is mastered should the couple practice the full *promenade*.

The best way to practice the *promenade* is to strike the pose as above and, having helped the girl to tilt forwards, the boy gives 'impetus' to the turn by starting the circle to the right with a firm step on his left foot. After completing the full circle, he helps the girl to return to her original *arabesque*.

Following the same principle as above, *promenades* should be practised in 2nd, 3rd and 4th *arabesques, attitudes,* etc.; see sketch 43. It is also most valuable for the boy to study this type of *promenade* holding the girl's waist, not only curving his arm above the hip, but also from underneath – compare sketches 42 and 43 to realise the difference.

There are other aspects of *promenades* when the boy holds the girl with one hand; see sketch 44. For example; the girl stands in *attitude croisée* on her right *pointe*, arms in 3rd. The boy faces her with his right arm curved round the back of her waist, finger-tips reaching her right side because his elbow is slightly bent. He stands on his right foot, left *pointe tendue derrière* with his body and head braced very slightly backwards. The boy then lowers the girl a little way away from himself as if she were 'resting' on his arm. The principle used is that described in the preceding *ports de bras*; see sketches 43 and 44. In this position, the boy can circle to the left by stepping forwards or backwards. At first only half a circle should be attempted; later a full circle and ultimately three, four or more. At the end of the *promenade* the boy must return the girl to her original pose and help her to restore her weight over her own centre of balance, i.e., the supporting leg.

43. 4th *arabesque*, the girl held by the boy's right hand from underneath

44. *Attitude croisée*, the boy's right hand round and behind the girl's waist

During a *promenade* in *écarté*, when the boy has one arm round the girl's waist, the partners must feel only one physical point of contact. They must know exactly where is the centre round which they both revolve and counter-poise their weights.

During all *promenades* when the boy is holding the girl with one hand, or has his arm on or round her body, he must never contract his fingers strongly nor hold her dress. Whether his hand is over or under her body, with a well-opened stretch between thumb and forefinger embracing the side of the girl's waist, its actual position always depends upon the girl's pose.

In certain classical *pas de deux, promenades* can be found where the partners face each other in the following position: the palm of the girl's right hand rests on her boy's right shoulder and his right palm rests on her right shoulder. The arms are thus interlocked; see sketch 45.

45. A hold in *attitude éffacée* with interlocked arms

## Pirouettes

**Ex. 1:** *Pirouettes* holding the girl with one hand – sketch 39.

The girl stands in *attitude éffacée* on her right *pointe*. The boy faces her holding her right hand in his right, palm to palm in 1st position. The girl with a *fondu sur la pointe* takes 'force' for a *pirouette en dedans*. At the moment when the hands are joined, the boy's right arm must be strong and resilient. Immediately the girl pushes away from his hand and begins to turn, he must immediately place both hands on her waist and help her to regain and retain her centre of balance during the pirouette. These pirouettes should be studied with and without the preliminary *fondu*.

**Ex. 2:** *Pirouettes* holding the girl by the waist with one hand – see sketches 40 and 46.

The girl stands in 1st *arabesque* (high) on her right *pointe* facing point 3. The boy stands facing her about one step away, holding her right wrist with his right hand. The girl does a *pirouette en dedans*, raising her right arm to 3rd and lowering her left into preparatory position. At the moment she takes 'force', the boy leads her right arm into the position over her head, i.e., 3rd, as smoothly but as strongly as possible, so that she immediately raises her body into the vertical position and is centrally balanced.

When the girl takes 'force', the boy's arm must be strongly resilient as she pushes away from him. At the moment when the turn begins he must NEVER SQUEEZE the girl's wrist. Her arm must be free to turn in his hand.

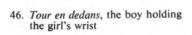

46. *Tour en dedans*, the boy holding the girl's wrist

41

If after the turn the girl again poses in 1st *arabesque*, the boy must return to the correct position, i.e., lower it from 3rd into 1st *arabesque*. He must do this smoothly and accurately the moment she completes the *pirouette* and opens her left leg into *arabesque*. After this finish, the girl should be able to hold her pose without the partner's help. If she takes too much 'force' for multiple turns, the boy must not try and stop her by squeezing her wrist. This squeeze can so easily lead to bad injuries.

When holding the girl's wrist in *pirouettes*, the boy can either face or stand behind her.

**Ex. 3:** *Pirouettes* during which the girl revolves round the boy's middle finger – see sketch 32.

N.B. Some dancers prefer the index finger. It is useful to teach how to use either so that boy and girl, when safely partnered, can decide for themselves which is the more comfortable.

The basic principles of these *pirouettes* have already been discussed (see p. 18). But if the girl has already placed her arm above her head before the *pirouette* begins and the boy is already standing behind her, holding her arm or hand, then before she begins her *pirouette*, the boy must re-set his and her fingers so that his middle finger points downwards and her fingers encircle it.

The quality and quantity of this type of *pirouette* depends entirely upon the boy's ability to maintain the axis round which the girl's hand turns and keep it firmly centred over her head.

These *pirouettes* must be studied commencing with a step, a *tombé*, *pas de bourrée* or other movement as a preparation from which the girl herself can take 'force'.

After such a *pirouette* the girl must learn to finish in all small and large poses of classical dance.

If the girl remains *sur la pointe*, i.e., without *fondu*, the boy as a rule can help her by taking her free arm or hand, or placing his free arm on her waist. If after the *pirouette* she sinks into *fondu* or *demi-plié*, the boy has no need to help and should not try.

**Ex. 4:** *Pirouette* and turn in *attitude*, during which the boy places his hand on the girl's waist – see sketch 47.

The girl stands *à la seconde* at 90° on her left *pointe*, arms in 2nd. The boy, standing to her right facing point 1, takes her right hand in his left, palm to palm. With a *fondu* on left, the girl pushes away from the boy's hand to take 'force' and makes a *pirouette en dehors* into *attitude* raising her arms to 3rd. The girl should make this turn for herself. The boy then takes a step forwards towards her on his right foot, and when her left shoulder approaches him he can place his right hand behind her body. She opens her left arm into 2nd and places it round the back of his shoulder.

As the boy nears the girl during the *pirouette* he must not stop her flow of movement but quickly ensure its continuity by moving forwards in a circle, i.e., *promenade*, so that the girl can finish in *attitude* *éffacée*. There are many variants to follow this *pirouette*: once the boy has embraced the girl as above, he can turn two, three, or more times; the girl's arm, bent at the elbow can rest on the boy's right shoulder; she can make a half turn for herself and then the boy can embrace her waist, etc.

47. *Tour in attitude*, boy's right arm cradled round back of girl's waist, her left arm round his shoulder

In this type of *pirouette* the boy must always approach the girl with care and NEVER 'knock into her' thus spoiling the axis on which she is turning. He must also move speedily into the circle and in the same tempo with which the girl began her turn. In other words he must accurately co-ordinate his simple circling walk with her swift turn *en place* without in any way distorting the general line both are making.

## SUPPORTED ADAGE INTO 'FALLING' POSITIONS AND POSES

**Ex. 1:** Lowering the girl into a 'falling' position from 1st *arabesque*, one arm round her waist (cradle hold) – see sketch 48.

The girl stands in 1st *arabesque* (high) on her left *pointe*. The boy, a little to her left, faces point 1 and places his right arm behind and round her body so that the tips of his fingers reach as far as her right hip. His left arm is opened to the side, palm downwards. His right foot is braced firmly against the girl's supporting toe. Holding the girl firmly, and as she rests her left hip against his right side, he smoothly lunges forwards to point 7 on his left foot and lowers her into the 'falling' position. As she 'falls' she must retain the straight *arabesque*, with which she began the movement, throughout her body.

The boy must return the girl to her original position solely with the help of his left leg and right side. From this final pose the teacher should make further additions.

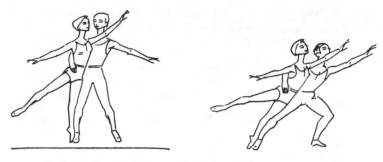

48. Lowering the girl into a 'falling' position held by one hand

**Ex. 2:** Both partners lower each other into the 'falling' position – see sketch 49.

The girl stands on the boy's right, both facing point 1. They link arms close together, her left arm under his right, the palm of her hand clasped over his. He must be careful how he moves his wrist slightly upwards. The joined hands rest on his waist. Their outside arms are in the preparatory position. The girl rises to 5th *sur les pointes*, right foot *devant*. The boy braces his right foot against the girl's left and draws his own left foot tightly against his right. (N.B. He is in 6th position.) At this moment both girl and boy, firmly holding hands and arms, gradually fall away from each other, counterpoising each other's weight.

To do this they begin to pull away and their outside arms gradually rise into 2nd, i.e., her right and his left. At the same time, she extends her left arm but he, without straightening his right elbow, smoothly presses her left hand against his chest as he raises it with his right hand. From this higher position he slowly extends his own right arm

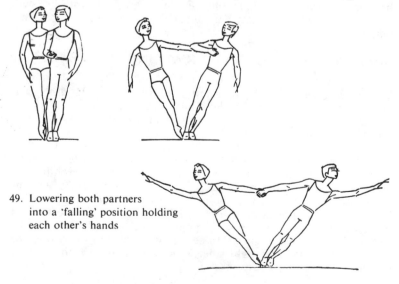

49. Lowering both partners into a 'falling' position holding each other's hands

and, when it is fully stretched, both partners will have reached the final position and should be counterbalancing each other.

To return to the preparatory position, the boy first draws his own hand back to his chest as he takes half a step sideways with his left foot and then draws the girl upwards into the vertical position as he lowers his right arm to his waist. At this moment, he quickly places both hands on her waist and she takes any pose determined by the teacher.

During the entire lowering of their bodies sideways, neither boy nor girl must slacken their pose in any way. They must remain with their spines fully stretched as well as their legs. During any similar movement in *pas de deux* the boy must aim to maintain his firm grip on the girl's hand in as natural a position as possible.

**Ex. 3:** Lowering the girl into a 'falling' position in 1st *arabesque* with one hand – see sketch 50.

The girl stands in 1st *arabesque* on her left *pointe*. The boy stands close behind her, the upturned palm of his left hand holding the down-turned palm of her right. His right elbow is bent and his forearm is at waist level. Having taken this preliminary position, the boy braces the instep of his right foot against the girl's left *pointe*. As he bends his right knee, i.e., *fondu*, and stretches his left leg outwards and diagonally forwards, his body inclines backwards as the girl stretches away from him. Simultaneously he releases her left arm and stretches his own right arm diagonally downwards and across his chest. His elbow must stretch slowly and co-ordinate with the outwards stretching of his left leg.

On returning to the preparatory position, the boy must draw his right arm and left foot strongly and smoothly backwards, reversing exactly the way into which he first stretched them. Once the girl has returned to *arabesque*, he can place his two hands on her waist, or on her two wrists, or as the teacher suggests.

50. Lowering the girl in 1st *arabesque* from one hand

PART II

# LIFTS IN THE AIR

## INTRODUCTION

When studying any form of lifts into the air, the first essential for the partners is their mutual agreement as to the timing and tempo of the movements to be made so that they absolutely co-ordinate these at the moment of the 'lift' or 'jump', no matter whether this is taken from a stationary position or a run or jump into the air. Timing means the degree of speed required to accomplish each detailed movement of the lift. In classical *pas de deux*, the partners' mutual feelings as they correctly time and co-ordinate their movements constitute the essence and quality of the lift. This is only achieved when they have acquired technical assurance, are properly prepared and can fully co-ordinate their movements with the phasing and tempo of the music. Only a full understanding of how to co-ordinate and co-operate with each other will preserve the lightness and purity of the lines of classical dance.

The teacher must protect the boys, particularly when growing, from undue strain when teaching any lift into the air. He must come to each lesson fully prepared to teach only a given amount of material suitable to the standards of those students in front of him. If the *enchâinements* include new examples of any lift, then before allowing any attempt to be made, he must explain what is required. First, he explains to the girl exactly what are her movements, her placing of the various parts of the body, the spacing of the movement and so on. Then he explains to the boy how to hold or catch and lift the girl. All this must be done because both partners must understand that the boy's action depends entirely upon how the girl initiates and performs the movement. After the first explanation of any new and difficult lift, it is essential that the teacher takes each couple individually.

The boy must maintain strict discipline and unswerving concentration during classes so that he cannot hurt the girl in any way by lacking attention to her needs through the slackening of his muscles, mistiming of movements, or slow reactions.

On no account must the partners be carried away enthusiastically by any prolonging or speeding up of the *enchâinements*, nor by overloading them with too many difficult lifts repeated four or five times. It is better to concentrate on perfecting the preparation, climax and finish of one or two lifts.

Before any study of difficult lifts and 'throws' into the air it is important to eliminate any sense of fear. (A 'throw' is when the boy tosses the girl upwards and then catches her.) To do this the girl must constantly be reminded that she must never change her position in the air, but remain absolutely still (fixed) in the same pose. The boy himself must feel confident as he lifts and later 'throws' her upwards. As a further safeguard, and always at the beginning of practice the teacher himself, or another boy, must stand ready in an appropriate

46

position and lend a hand to give confidence to the girl. These appropriate positions are noted in all exercises mentioned later, when a 'throw' is to be used.

Before lifting the girl on to his shoulder or chest, or on fully stretched arms, the boy must not bend his body in any way backwards from the waist. His spine must always be straight but never stiffened because his waist-line and knees are very vulnerable if he departs from the strictly classical rule of keeping his own weight firmly centred over his own feet. He should remember he is not a weight-lifter – he is dealing with a live body who will respond to any straining backwards, usually by doing likewise. If this happens, the weight of the girl's body is equally displaced, to the detriment of the lift and both his and her spines.

When boy students are practising lifts in class they must proceed no further than their own physical strength allows. It is essential first to lift the girl making use of the strength of her own jump. In this way the boy keeps something of his own muscular strength in reserve to use when higher lifts are required.

The teacher should never allow any growing boy to practise difficult lifts on his own until satisfied that he is able to do these correctly in class.

The ballet world divides its girl dancers into two divisions for double-work: those who are 'comfortable' and those who are 'uncomfortable' and heavy: but LIGHT does not always mean 'comfortable'. In a word, 'comfortable' implies that a girl possesses good professional talents such as an understanding of the rules, lines and forms of classical dance; who is quick to react, is a brave and trustworthy partner responding immediately to the demands of the movement, as she coordinates with the strength and dexterity of her partner and the music.

During every lesson the girl must fulfil each given movement in exact accordance with those same rules of classical dance which apply to solo work. She is responsible for seeing that all her muscles are fully attuned and active and respond to the demands made by her partner and the step.

If the girl is upheld in her partner's fully stretched arms, she must not correct nor neaten her pose. If she does she will upset the delicate balance and counterpoise of their positions and thus her own and her partner's equilibrium. She MUST REMAIN STILL.

The signal to begin a lift should be imperceptible to the audience but distinct to each partner. It depends entirely on the preparation or hold taken and used. The signal must be decided upon and clearly understood by the partners themselves. The principal quality to be displayed during any lift in the air is the effortless ease with which both partners co-ordinate their movements as they commence, accomplish and complete the lift.

The girl must always calculate the spacing of her run or jump exactly so that she never 'flies' past her partner. The highest point of her jump (i.e., trajectory) must finish in his arms, or on his shoulders, chest or elsewhere.

By following all the above-mentioned rules as well as those in the first part of this book, the girl will make the boy's task so much easier and lighten the physical strain that all lifts in classical dance confer on his body.

## LITTLE JUMPS AND SMALL LIFTS TO THE LEVEL OF THE CHEST OR SHOULDER

All types of *petit elevation*, without any exception, must be studied in *pas de deux*. The most important are: *temps levés, sauts, changements de pieds, assemblés, jetés, jetés entrelacés, sissonnes, sissonnes fermées, sissonnes fondues, soubresauts, pas de chat, pas de basque, cabrioles*, etc. They must be studied and used as they are in solo dance in their five forms, i.e., from two feet to two feet; two feet to one; one foot to two; one foot to the other, and all on one foot. The boy can hold the girl with both hands on her waist, hold her hands, or wrists, hold her under her shoulders, or with only one hand.

The boy must aim at keeping his lifts looking easy and light and lower the girl softly to the floor.

Every jump must begin with a *demi-plié* or *fondu*. Every *demi-plié* made by the girl is the signal for the boy to be alert. He lightly but firmly places his hands on her body as if to help her with her *demi-plié* as he simultaneously bends his knees as the girl bends hers. He must remember to lift her UPWARDS only and never push her forwards away from himself and, at the same time, NEVER push his own weight backwards.

After any jump with a change of feet, the girl should always make a slight change of *épaulement*. The boy must co-ordinate his movement with this slight change in order to help the girl move into the correct direction and position as she lands.

During any *temps levé sauté*, the boy must understand how to carry the girl forwards, sideways or backwards during the jump and NOT when it begins.

During any *sissonnes fermées, pas ballonnés*, etc., where the movements travel forwards, sideways or backwards, the boy must travel with the girl and lower her softly to the floor in a 'held' position after each jump. When holding the girl during *pas ballonnés* the boy should not as a rule be behind the girl, but should be just to her left or right side.

## JUMPS HOLDING THE GIRL WITH BOTH HANDS ON HER WAIST

**Ex. 1:** *Changements de pieds* – see sketch 51.

The girl is in 5th position, right foot *devant*; her arms are in preparatory position. The boy is behind her in 2nd, both hands on her waist. Simultaneously with the girl's *demi-plié*, he bends his knees and, without slackening his hold on her waist, turns the palms of his hands so that his fingers incline more upwards – see hands in sketches 51 and 52. This position of the boy's hands is characteristic for most lifts and jumps when holding the girl's waist with both hands. The girl does *changements de pieds* as the boy lifts and softly lowers her to the floor. N.B. The boy must NEVER allow his hands to slip upwards or forwards because they must never touch the girl's breast.

**Ex. 2:** *Pas assemblé* (travelling sideways) – see sketch 52.

The girl is in 5th position, right foot *derrière*, arms in preparatory position. The boy is behind her close to her right shoulder, both hands on her waist.

Simultaneously both girl and boy *glissade* diagonally to point 2. The girl continues into *assemblé*, the boy lifting her and carrying her towards point 2, holding her in his hands and then softly lowering her to the floor in 5th position.

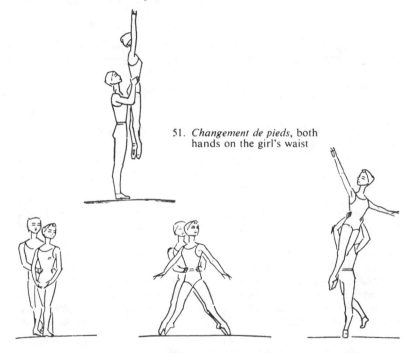

51. *Changement de pieds*, both hands on the girl's waist

52. *Grand assemblé*, both hands on the girl's waist

**Ex. 3:** *Sissonne* with a lift in 1st *arabesque* – see sketch 53.

The girl is in 5th position, right foot *devant*, arms in 1st position. The boy is behind her, both hands on her waist. Simultaneously, both move into *demi-plié* and he changes his hands on her waist-line, his right hand a little forwards and downwards, the fingers slightly upwards, left hand just behind and a little higher towards the girl's left shoulder, also turning the fingers upwards. This position of the hands allows the girl to hold 1st *arabesque* correctly in the air as she is lifted. The boy must lift her directly into the jump as he rises from the *demi-plié* and steps on to the right foot. He then lowers her softly to the floor, still in 1st *arabesque* on right *pointe*.

During the first attempts at this lift the boy must not lift the girl very high. It is more important to increase the length of the jump. The boy's hand movement in this jump is characteristic for later lifts into *grand jeté*, *sissonnes*, *soubresauts*, *cabrioles* into 1st, 2nd, 3rd and 4th *arabesques*.

53. *Sissonne* into 1st *arabesque*, both hands on the girl's waist

## JUMPS WITH A LIFT FROM TWO HANDS USING VARIOUS HOLDS

**Ex. 1:** *Grand assemblé* holding the girl's hand with one hand, the other on her side at the waist-line – see sketch 54.

The girl stands on her right foot in 1st *arabesque à terre* facing point 2. The boy is behind her about one step away in the same pose. He holds her left hand in his left, palm to palm, his underneath, his right arm in 3rd. The girl *pas chassé tombé* on left foot into *grand assemblé* towards point 6, only jumping upwards. As the girl commences *chassé*, the boy places his right hand on her left side (fingers upwards) and immediately moves with her into the *chassé*. After this, he takes a large step forwards with his left foot and, with a half turn, finishes the movement with a strong movement on his right foot. Simultaneously with the *assemblé*, the boy straightens his right elbow and pushes the girl into the air away from himself; his left arm must

54. *Grand assemblé*, one hand on the girl's waist,
   the other holding her hand

not be held too strongly bent at the elbow, but it must be firm enough to give the girl confidence to hold herself straight. By using his arms correctly in all such lifts, the boy will be able to lower the girl softly.

**Ex. 2:** *Grand assemblé* round the boy, who holds the girl with both hands – see sketch 55.

The preparation can be the same as in Ex. 1. The girl then turns to face her partner and raises her right arm to 3rd, placing the palm of her hand over his. The boy also turns his right wrist so that the palm is upwards as she places her hand on his. Their left hands are joined palm to palm in 1st; see sketch 55. After a *sissonne tombée* on her left foot, the girl moves into *grand assemblé*. At this moment the girl's right foot brushes behind the boy's back towards point 3 so that the *assemblé* will finish correctly.

Simultaneously with the girl rising from the floor, the boy must raise both arms upwards in order to help the girl jump and turn in the air round himself (so to speak). After this, he inclines his body forwards a little to help the girl to descend softly. The girl must be careful at the moment of flight not to travel too far behind the boy.

In this exercise, the girl must finish in 5th position, right foot *devant*, then make a *tour soutenu* to the left during which the boy takes her arm through all three positions, thus helping her to turn.

In later studies of *assemblé* round the boy, the partners can commence from three to four steps away from each other, taking hands only at the moment of meeting. In these cases the approach to each other can be *pas chassé*, *pas de bourrée*, etc., but before the *assemblé* there must always be a strong *pas tombé*.

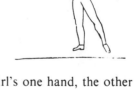

55. *Grand assemblé* round the partner, holding both hands

**Ex. 3:** *Jeté entrelacé*, the boy holding the girl's one hand, the other on her hip – see sketch 56.

The preparation for this exercise is the same as in Ex. 1. The girl *pas chassé tombé* and then *jeté entrelacé* in a diagonal from point 2 to 6. Simultaneously with her *chassé*, the boy places his right hand on her right hip, the tips of his fingers directed downwards. The girl's and boy's left hands are joined and both in 1st position. At the moment of the jump, the boy's right hand tries to thrust the girl's body higher as his left hand serves as a lever to her left arm. The boy then strongly holds both arms in this position to lower the girl softly. The *jeté entrelacé* can finish in 2nd *arabesque* or *attitude éffacée*.

The above examples of lifts are of great value when studying *fouetté sauté en tournant* finishing in *attitude* and other studies. The preparatory positions should be as varied as possible once the principle of such travelling jumps has been mastered.

56. *Jeté entrelacé*, one hand holding the girl's hands, the other under her thigh

**Ex. 4:** The boy turns the girl from *attitude éffacée* into a horizontal position in his arms – see sketch 57.

The girl stands in *attitude éffacée* on her left *pointe*, left arm resting behind the boy's shoulders. The boy faces point 1 on the girl's left, his right arm cradled round and behind her body, finger-tips on her right hip, left arm in 2nd, The girl *fondu* left and *grand battement jété*, right foot, with a jump towards point 7, allowing the body to fall into a horizontal position, back to the floor and at the same time bringing her left leg to the right in 5th position. Immediately the girl does *grand battement*, the boy slips his right arm further round her waist and lifts her as his right arm quickly cradles over her right side, his left hand firmly holding her thighs just above the knees. At the same time, he, lunges on to his right foot.

57. Change from *attitude éffacée* into the horizontal position

As the girl moves into the horizontal, she must not deviate to any corner nor regain her vertical position, but immediately tilt her body backwards into a straight line the moment her right leg brushes forwards. The boy can then use the strength of both arms to lift her upwards again, as with a swift movement he changes his own centre of balance on his left leg and turns the girl's body to finish with her back to point 7 as he lowers her to the floor in 5th *sur les pointes*. Her feet must rest on the inner side of his left foot. The girl's stance must be firmly established throughout the whole exercise.

## JUMPS WITH ONE-HAND HOLDS

On the stage *pas de deux* with the boy using one hand only is often seen, in particular the boy holding the girl's hand or wrist. Therefore during training both girl and boy must be given many varied *enchâinements* using this particular form of lift.

**Ex. 1:** *Pas sissonne* in 1st *arabesque* using one hand.

The girl stands in 5th position, right foot *devant*, arms in preparatory position. The boy is behind her in the same pose. Both simultaneously *pas sissonne tombé* on right foot. The girl continues into *sissonne* in 1st *arabesque*. At this moment, the boy takes her right wrist in his right hand, the girl moving into *failli*, *pas assemblé* into 5th, or another step.

**Ex. 2:** *Grand fouetté sauté*, the boy helping with one hand – see sketch 58.

The girl is in 1st *arabesque à terre* (or *en l'air*) facing point 8 on her left foot (or *pointe*). The boy is about one step behind her, his right hand holding her right (palm to palm). He pulls her towards him and she, with *pas chassé* diagonally to point 4, continues into *fouetté sauté* turning into *attitude croisée*. At the moment of the jump, she pushes her arm away from his to increase the size of her jump. The height of her right arm must not change.

58. *Grand fouetté sauté* holding one hand

## SMALL LIFTS

**Ex. 1:** From a 'falling' position.

The girl is in 5th position, right foot *devant*, arms in 3rd. The boy is behind her. Having lowered the girl in cradle hold on his right arm – see sketch 48 – the boy places his left arm over her right hip and raises her so that she returns to the horizontal position in his arms; see sketch 57. After this he replaces her on the floor in the same way as mentioned above.

**Ex. 2:** Lift in 1st *arabesque* – see sketch 59.

The girl stands in 1st *arabesque* on her right *pointe*. The boy is behind her, both hands on her body. His right arm is cradled under her waist so that her supporting leg is firmly centred just in front of his right hip (he is in a lunge on his right leg) but his left arm is holding her left thigh above the knee and just above his own left hip. Then, stretching both legs upwards, he lifts the girl so that he holds her weight directly over his right leg. Simultaneously with the lift, she bends her right knee so that her toe is pointed close in front or behind her left ankle. The boy must not alter the girl's placing in any way when he lifts her. During the lift she must hold her body strongly and still and turn her head slightly backwards.

59. Lift in 1st *arabesque*

Returning the girl to the original position must be performed in the following way: the boy retains the weight of the girl's body over his right leg and begins to lower her, but at the same time she must stretch her right leg downwards. He can then replace her on her right *pointe* without bending his body forwards. Only when she is safely balanced on the floor can he place his hands on her waist, left first, then the right.

**Ex. 3:** 'Swallow' on the boy's hip – see sketch 60.

The girl is in 1st *arabesque* and is lifted as in Ex. 2, but the boy is on his left leg. As he draws it backwards, he balances the girl on his left thigh and stretches his right leg forwards towards point 2. At the moment when the boy lifts the girl, she bends her right leg to her left and takes the 'swallow' pose. Her pelvis should rest squarely on his left thigh and he must adjust his body so that she can curve round his left side and not in front of him. (In the sketch, the girl has a good deal of strain in her back as her weight is too far forwards.)

The girl's legs must be strongly bent at the knees, and her ankles pressed behind on to the boy's left shoulder blade. Once he feels the pressure of the girl's body against his, he must incline it backwards so that it is impossible for her to tilt or slide forwards. At the begin-

60. 'Swallow' on the boy's thigh

ning of training his arms must continue to hold her body. Later he can open them, first the left arm to the side, and then the right to the front.

When returning the girl to her original pose, the boy must cradle his right hand under her waist and his left arm on her left thigh. As she straightens both legs, he replaces her on the floor in 1st *arabesque*.

**Ex. 4:** 1st *arabesque* on the boy's hip – see sketch 61

The girl stands with her back to point 4 on her left foot, right *pointe tendue devant*, right arm in 2nd and left in 1st, palms down. The boy stands in front of her about two steps away. He bends his right knee towards the girl's right side. His right arm is in 3rd, his left in 2nd, palm down. His right thigh must be perpendicular to the diagonal running between points 4–8. The girl steps on to her right foot and then places her left foot on the boy's right thigh close to his body and stands in 1st *arabesque*. He places both hands on her body so that the right embraces the back of her waist and the left is on her right thigh.

This pose can also be taken with the boy holding both the girl's hands; see sketch 62, and note the position of the hands, how the boy's position has changed, and how the centre line of balance is maintained.

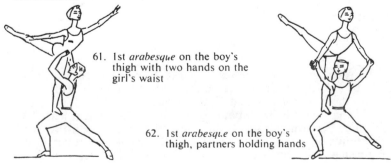

61. 1st *arabesque* on the boy's thigh with two hands on the girl's waist

62. 1st *arabesque* on the boy's thigh, partners holding hands

If the girl springs on to the boy's thigh in 1st *arabesque*, it is better that she prepares with *pas couru* or *glissade* before the *jeté*. She must spring or jump and land close to the boy's thigh in such a way that she can control her own movement and balance herself before he takes her hands or waist.

If the girl does spring on to the boy's thigh, he cannot bend his knee beforehand but merely takes a large lunge so that his thigh and body are in the correct position. His left foot must still be directed towards point 6 if she is jumping on to the right thigh, but to point 2 if she is jumping on to his right thigh from the other angle.

The girl can be lowered to the floor in many different ways. For example: the girl, standing on the boy's thigh, can use a *passé* into *pose éffacée* (right leg) then fall on to the right leg towards point 2 and finish the movement in 1st or 2nd *arabesque*. The boy, holding both hands on her body helps to descend softly. Or the girl, standing on the boy's thigh can hold her 1st *arabesque* and 'fall' towards point 8 as he cradles his left arm under her body and his right over her thigh. He can then lower her to the floor.

**Ex. 5:** The 'fish' into the boy's arms – see sketch 63.

The girl sits on the floor facing point 2, her left foot stretched forwards; see sketch 38, but note that the girl is using her right foot. The boy stands about two steps away in a pose selected by the teacher. He lunges towards the girl on his left foot and offers her his right hand, palm upwards. She places her right hand on his right palm; a wrist grip can also be used. He gives a pull from his shoulder and draws the girl upwards towards himself. As she rises from the floor, she moves first on to the left and then the right foot. Immediately after this jump, the boy catches her in his arms and holds her in 'fish' by cradling his right arm under her body and holding her left hip in his left hand; compare this 'fish' with sketch 60.

63. 'Fish' in the boy's arms

The foregoing 'fish' requires a markedly backwards pull of the girl's arm which must be made on the beat of the music. This signal ensures the co-ordination and simultaneous timing for both boy and girl. The girl must NOT initiate nor hinder the movement herself by tightening her arm, nor by bending her wrist during the lift to 'fish'.

This lift can also be studied with the girl turning in the air so that she finishes in the boy's arms with her spine to the floor.

## HALF TURNS WITH A 'THROW' INTO THE AIR

In turns of a similar type as that mentioned above the boy must turn the girl TOWARDS himself but never FROM himself. That mentioned below is the simplest to be found during early training.

**Ex.:** From 1st *arabesque* in the partner's arm.

The girl is in 1st *arabesque* on her right *pointe* facing point 3 and does *fondu* as the boy, bending his knees slightly and easily, 'throws' her upwards in a turn. At that moment, she must sharply raise her arms to 3rd and bring her right foot into 5th and make a full turn by drawing the left shoulder backwards and towards the boy, keeping her body absolutely straight and horizontal to the floor. The boy must catch her as she finishes by cradling his left arm over her right thigh and his right under her waist. He can then return the girl to the floor as in sketch 57.

This turn and its recovery should be studied with other poses, particularly studying how to return the girl from the horizontal position to the floor in 1st *arabesque*.

## JUMPS INTO THE BOY'S ARMS

**Ex. 1:** *Jeté entrelacé* into the boy's arms finishing in 'fish'.

The girl stands in 1st *arabesque* facing point 2. The boy is behind her about two steps away, in a diagonal from points 2–6 in any pose decided by the teacher. The girl: *pas chassé tombé* on her left foot and *jeté entrelacé* towards point 6. Simultaneously, the boy transfers his centre line of balance on to his right foot and stretches his right arm forwards, and, turning the palm of his hand upwards, catches the girl so that the ends of his fingers are on the left side of her pelvis. With his left hand, he thus holds her left thigh. The girl must control and calculate the spacing of her jump so that it finishes in the boy's arms.

The clarity of the *jeté entrelacé* depends solely on the lightness and purity of the partners' co-ordination, and the timing of their movements. This needs a great deal of practice.

**Ex. 2:** Jump into the boy's arms, finishing in a horizontal position, spine to the floor – see sketch 64.

The girl stands with her back to point 3 on her left foot, pose *croisé devant à terre*. The boy faces point left and about three to four

64. The moment of the jump in horizontal
position

steps away in a straight line from points 3–7, in a pose decided by the teacher. The girl moves towards the boy: *glissade, posé* right and strongly throwing her left leg upwards from the floor, rises into the horizontal position, raising her arms to 3rd. On arriving in this position, the girl must hold it strongly in a straight line. Her spine must not curve backwards nor slacken in any way. Simultaneously with the *glissade*, the boy lunges on to his right foot, inclining his body towards the girl and cradling his right arm under her waist as he catches her and moves his left hand over her right thigh.

During the first attempts at this lift, the girl can curve her left arm round the boy's shoulders, embracing his neck, as it were.

The jump should be studied with various preparations: *pas de bourrée, pas couru*, etc. The girl's every step must be calculated for size and distance so that she does not 'fly past' the boy.

**Ex. 3:** *Grand fouetté sauté* into the boy's arms, finishing in 'fish' – see sketch 65.

The preparation is the same as in Ex. 2. The girl: *glissade* and 'throw' the left leg towards point 7 in *grand fouetté sauté*, finishing in 1st *arabesque*. The boy catches her in the air, his right arm under her body and his left over her left thigh. The girl holds both arms in 'fish' position.

65. *Grand fouetté-sauté* to the partner

It is very important that in this jump the girl finishes her *fouetté* in the air as if continuing her flight on to the boy's back. At the finish of the jump, her shoulder blades MUST be pressed firmly against his chest.

**Ex. 4:** *Grand jeté* into the boy's arms, the pose being caught and held with one hand embracing the girl's body – see sketches 66 and 67.

The girl stands in the furthest corner of the stage back to point 4 on her left foot, *pose croisée devant à terre*. The boy is in the centre of the stage, facing the girl from four to five steps away from her, in any pose decided by the teacher. The girl: *pas couru, jeté en attitude* to point 8. She must control both her preparation and jump so that she finishes her 'flight' in her partner's arms. As the girl commences *pas couru*, the boy lunges on to his right foot and stretches his right arm forwards ready to catch the 'flying' girl by the waist, his left arm remaining in 2nd position. On arriving in the boy's arm, the girl

66. *Grand jeté* into 2nd *arabesque*, one hand round the girl's waist

67. Variation to the finishing position after *grand jeté*

places her left arm across the back of his neck and presses it against both shoulders; see sketch 66. Having caught the girl, the boy moves diagonally towards point 8, making two, three or more turns.

The movement can then finish in 2nd *arabesque fondu*, the boy lightly guiding the girl to the floor with his left hand. Alternatively, during the last turn the girl can bring her right foot to the left and the boy sits her on his right knee; see sketch 67.

**Ex. 5:** The girl, with a run, jumps into the boy's arm, finishing in 'fish' – sketch 68.

The girl stands in the furthest corner of the stage back to point 6 in any pose decided by the teacher. The boy is in the centre of the stage facing her from five to six steps away in a similar pose. The girl runs and with a *petit assemblé* right foot, a few steps from the boy springs upwards from both feet and flies towards the boy assuming the 'fish' pose. The jump must be made with such precision and impetus that its height will be as high as the boy's shoulders. The trajectory of the flight must finish exactly in his arms. As the girl jumps, the boy lunges on his left leg and stretches his right arm forwards, catching the girl under her waist in cradle hold and placing his left hand on her left thigh. Having caught the girl, he immediately transfers his weight on

59

68. Jump ending in 'fish'

to his right leg, thus holding and softening the girl's flight. The distance between girl and boy can be increased as their expertise grows.

When beginning to study this form of jump, it can be made from two feet, that is, from *assemblé*. Later, it should be practised with *pas sissonne*. This should be tried with the girl facing the boy about one step away, the boy's hand being placed under the girl's torso.

The same form of jump can also be practised with the girl making a turn into the horizontal position, i.e., back to the floor. The girl, as she jumps, makes a full turn to the left, the boy catching her with his right arm under her waist and his left on her right thigh; see sketch 69. This jump is seldom studied to the opposite side. The boy must always be careful how he transfers his weight from his left to his right leg, and be certain that his body follows the line of the girl's flight downwards.

69. Jump in horizontal position ending with the back to the floor

60

## GRAND ELEVATION WITH LIFTS ON TO THE CHEST AND SHOULDERS

In those circumstances when the girl's pose has to be firmly fixed on the boy's chest or shoulders, it is essential that both girl and boy acquire the habit of holding absolutely still and erect, whether moving in a circle or turning *en place* three or more times.

**Ex. 1:** Lifting the girl on to the chest or shoulder into 'sitting' position – see sketch 70.

The girl stands in 5th position, right foot *devant*, arms in preparatory position. The boy is behind her, hands on her waist. The girl rises *sur les pointes*, holding her position, and just opens her arms sideways; then gently bends both knees into *demi-plié* and jumps up strongly. The movement must be as strong as that used for any *changement de pieds*. Simultaneously with the jump she raises her arms to 3rd. Later the arms can be varied and as decided by the teacher.

70. 'Sitting' on the partner's chest

The boy co-ordinates his *demi-plié* with that of the girl and, as she jumps, must lift her strongly. Then, taking a step forwards, he places her on his chest, changing his arms and elbows so that they are gripping her thighs, the palms of his hands holding the front part of her waist; see sketch 70.

In order to achieve the 'sitting' position, the girl must hold her waist very strongly, her spine absolutely straight, and must NEVER incline her head forwards. She can then open her right leg forwards at 90° (*croisé*), with the left leg slightly bent at the knee and pressed firmly against the boy's right side; it can also be quite straight.

The boy must replace his hands on the girl's waist before he softly lowers her to the floor. She must straighten her body and guide both legs slightly forwards; then slide down the boy's chest, thus returning to the floor on one or two feet.

The principle of lifting the girl on to the shoulder is the same as above; see sketch 71. Before a lift on to the right shoulder, both the boys hands are usually placed to the right so that his left hand is a little further forwards and upwards on the girl's left side when the lift takes place. If the lift is to be on the left shoulder, then the left hand is on the waist and the right hand a little higher on her right side. If the girl is in a tunic or very full skirt, then he must not squeeze his fingers or elbows, for this would destroy the line of her costume when he lifts her on to his chest or shoulder.

**Ex. 2:** Lifting the girl on to the shoulder, finishing in *attitude allongée* – sketch 72.

The preparation is the same as in Ex. 1. As the girl jumps, the boy lifts her upwards with both hands, at the same time taking a step forwards on his left foot and placing her on his right shoulder. His right arm cradles round her body, his fingers reaching as far as possible round her right thigh. His left hand is directed towards her left hip. He inclines his head to the left so that it is pressed against her body. The girl should take the pose as she rises on to the boy's shoulder. Her left leg is bent at the knee but NOT turned out. Her left hip rests on the boy's shoulder and rests under her own right leg, her toe just above the left ankle.

Once the lift has been mastered, the boy must hold the girl with his right arm only, and open his left into 2nd position.

71. 'Sitting' on the partner's shoulder

72. *Attitude allongée* on the partner's shoulder

**Ex. 3:** Lifting the girl on to the shoulder with both hands – sketch 73.

The girl stands on right *pointe*, left *retiré croisé devant* and pointing to point 3. Her right arm is in the 1st position, palm down, and left is in 2nd, the back of her hand directed towards point 1 and stretched to its limit. The boy is to the left of the girl facing point 1, with palm of his right hand upwards, holding her right wrist firmly. The girl's left hand is in his left, palms together. His left elbow is bent.

The boy kneels on his right knee as near to the girl's right *pointe* as possible, but without changing the relationship of his shoulders to point 1, and places his right shoulder under her right thigh. She sits

62

73. Lift on to the shoulder,
using both hands

on his shoulder. Her spine must be absolutely straight, both arms fully stretched and held strongly, but with her head slightly turned and inclined to the left.

The lift must be achieved only through the strength of the boy pushing upwards from the floor with both legs. His body must be absolutely straight. When first studying this lift, the heights of the partners and the length of the girl's legs are particularly important. No very tall boy should lift a girl so short that he has to incline his body.

There are several ways of lowering the girl to the floor from this lift. The boy can again kneel on his right knee, the girl thus returning to her right *pointe*. The boy can lunge on to his right foot sideways and slightly incline his body in the same direction; the girl then slides from his shoulder and lightly springs to the floor in 5th *demi-plié*.

**Ex. 4:** Lifting the girl on to the shoulder with a turn into the horizontal position – see sketch 74.

The girl stands in 5th position *sur les pointes*, left foot *devant*, arms in 3rd. The boy is behind her, kneeling on his right knee, his right arm curved round behind her body, his left in 2nd position. The girl falls backwards and lies with her waist across his right shoulder. In this position, the boy stretches both legs and lifts the girl straight upwards. If he needs to steady and maintain the girl's horizontal position, then he must place his left hand under her left thigh and direct her feet to the correct point.

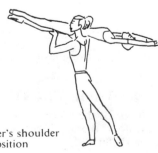

74. Lying on the partner's shoulder
in the horizontal position

A variation: the girl is in 'fish' in the boy's arms; see sketch 60. He lifts her with both hands towards himself and on to his right shoulder, so that her waist rests there. He would naturally have to change his grip and feel her bring her right foot to her left.

In the theatre, one meets these types of positions a great deal, particularly where the girl rests or stands on the boy's shoulder in some pose or another and he can then hold her with both hands on her waist or body, or with both hands, or with one hand on the body, or holding with one hand only. Such lifts must be studied as much as possible as the following suggests.

**Ex. 5:** Lifting the girl so that she finishes kneeling on the boy's shoulder – see sketch 75.

The girl stands facing point 1 in a convenient pose. The boy is on her right, kneeling on his right knee, also in some convenient pose. He gives her both hands, his right in 3rd and his left in 2nd, both palms upwards. She places her right hand in his and her left in his left, palms down. She then steps on to his left thigh so that her lower (left) leg and foot are against his body. Then, pressing on both his hands, she raises her right knee and kneels on his right shoulder as she opens her left leg backwards into 1st *arabesque*. Her arms must be fully stretched and strongly held at the elbows and wrists. As he rises and turns to face point 2, he straightens both arms at the elbows and holds them strongly uplifted. The boy must begin to turn before she raises and places her knee on his shoulder.

75. 1st *arabesque*, kneeling on the
partner's shoulder holding both hands

The girl can be returned to the floor in different ways. The most useful is as follows: the boy lunges on to his right foot and the girl lowers her left, as she stretches her right leg into 3rd *arabesque* as her left toe reaches the floor.

## JUMPS ON TO THE CHEST OR SHOULDER

The preparations for the following three examples are the same. The girl sits on the floor, the boy takes her hands as explained in Ex. 5 of small lifts; see sketch 38.

**Ex. 1:** The girl jumps on to the boy's shoulders in the horizontal position – sketch 76.

The boy pulls the girl towards himself with a sharp, strong movement as he inclines forwards. His body and left leg must be in an absolutely straight line. The girl strongly pushes off from the floor with her right foot and, during her jump, makes a half-turn to the left with such precision that her buttocks land on the boy's shoulder. Her body must be stretched into the horizontal position, her arms in 3rd, her legs stretched outwards in 5th, with right foot *devant*. The boy guides and then holds her on his right shoulder, immediately cradling his right arm round her waist and placing his left hand under her left thigh. At the moment when the girl arrives on the boy's shoulder, his legs must spring to 'attention' to withstand the strength of her jump and the weight of her body. He can then direct the line of her pose to any point decided by the teacher. The girl's body must remain absolutely still and straight and NEVER GIVE AT THE WAIST.

**Ex. 2:** The girl jumps on to the boy's shoulder in a 'sitting' position – sketch 77.

In the following examples, the boy helps the girl to spring into the air as above. She turns to the right during the jump and sits on his right shoulder (i.e., she turns towards the boy). Her arms are raised in 3rd position, legs bent at the knee in 6th position, i.e., NOT TURNED-OUT. The girl's body and both hips and knees must all face the same direction. The boy's right arm holds her right side; his left is in front of her left side, fingers upwards, and he turns to face point 1, straightening his knees.

77. 'Sitting' on the partner's shoulder

76. Lying horizontal on the partner's shoulder

**Ex. 3:** The girl jumps on to the boy's shoulder, finishing in 'swallow' –see sketch 78.

To perform this lift from the floor, the girl should push off strongly with her right foot as the boy pulls her right arm with his right. He then puts his left arm round her waist (she is in 'swallow' flight) and, simultaneously taking her right wrist in his right hand, brings her to rest on his left shoulder. He must make a turn clockwise so that she will finish in 'swallow' fully stabilised, the boy facing point 1. He

78. Jump on to the partner's shoulder, ending in 'swallow'

can then place his right hand just above the right side of her waist and take two or three steps forwards in the direction of the jump, thus giving the audience the illusion of a greater, longer flight.

**Ex. 4:** The girl jumps on to the boy's shoulder, finishing in 'sitting' position, using two hand holds – sketch 79.

The girl stands with her back to point 8 on her right foot in *pose croisé à terre*. Her left arm is in 3rd, palms towards the boy, right in 1st, palm down. The boy faces the girl on his left foot, right stretched backwards, arms in the same position as the girl's. He takes her right hand in his right, and her left in his left, palms facing palms. The girl: *pas couru* with left foot towards his spine and push off with right foot from the floor, jumping strongly and pressing herself upwards on his hands. During the jump, she bends her left knee and raises it to 90° (NOT TURNED-OUT). She must calculate and control the jump in such a way that her left buttock finally rests on the boy's right shoulder in the 'sitting' position. As the girl jumps, she must pass directly behind the boy's spine as at the same moment with a swift movement he catches her and lifts his arms upwards. Only when she is firmly 'sitting' on his shoulders must he fully stretch his legs. The return to the floor is accomplished as in Ex. 4, p. 82.

79. Jump on to the partner's shoulder finishing 'sitting' there, using both hands

66

**Ex. 5:** The girl jumps, and finishes kneeling on the boy's shoulder – sketch 80.

The preparation is the same as in Ex. 4 above but the boy does not turn, he brings his right foot forwards. The girl steps on to her left foot, *glissade* and pushing her left foot from the floor, behind the boy's spine, jumps on to his right shoulder by bending her right knee and stretching the left down behind. The descent from this lift is the same as in Ex. 4, p. 82.

80. Finish of jump to finish 'kneeling' on the partner's shoulder

**Ex. 6:** *Jeté entrelacé* on to the boy's shoulder with two hands hold - sketch 81.

The girl stands with her back to point 2 on her right foot, left *pointe tendue devant*. Her right arm is in 3rd, palm towards the boy, her left in 1st, palm down. The boy faces her on his right foot, left stretched backwards. His arms are in the same position as hers. He takes her hands in his, palm to palm. With a step on to her left foot, the girl *jeté entrelacé* in a diagonal towards point 6, aiming at resting the centre of her right thigh exactly on the boy's left shoulder, leaning her body lightly against his neck. She then brings her left leg towards her right very swiftly and stabilizes her pose in the 'swallow'. When making this jump, the girl must not 'fly' past the boy, otherwise she will rest either her waist or her stomach on his shoulder, and NOT HER PELVIS. This is essential if the pose is to be held.

81. *Jeté entrelacé* on to the partner's shoulder, holding both hands

As the girl jumps, the boy must bend slightly without thrusting his left shoulder backwards, and give a sharp pull and thrust of his arms upwards and very slightly forwards, raising them fully only when he feels the girl is firmly fixed on his shoulder. He must continue to hold her firmly with both hands and keep his spine absolutely straight.

To replace the girl on the floor, the boy kneels on his right knee. She lowers first one leg and then the other leg to stand on the floor in 5th position behind him. If the girl has rested on the boy's right shoulder, he should kneel on the left knee.

The jump on to the shoulder from a *jeté entrelacé* should be studied using one hand only. Moreover, more advanced students should practise taking the pose from various other poses and preparations. If the girl moves into the jump from a run, or both boy and girl move round each other, their hands should only just join before the jump,so that the pull from the boy's arm and the push of the girl's foot from the floor are given the greatest impetus.

**Ex. 7:** *Jeté entrelacé* on to the boy's shoulder, holding the girl with one hand on the hip and the other round her waist.

The preparation is the same as in the preceding example, but the boy does not hold the girl's hands. He stands facing her about two steps away. Girl: *pas chassé*, left foot into a sharp *tombé* on the left into *jeté entrelacé* towards point 6 and on to the boy's left shoulder. As the girl does *pas chassé*, the boy stretches his right arm forwards, fingers upwards, and holds her by the waist. As she brushes her right foot upwards, he catches her by curving his right arm below both her thighs and without thrusting his left shoulder backwards. When the 'swallow' has been stabilised on her shoulder he straightens his legs and turns to face point 8. The method of returning the girl to the floor has already been suggested in earlier examples.

In this lift, it should be noted that the boy places his right hand round the girl's waist if she rests on his right shoulder, but his left if on the left shoulder. But the boy must make a full turn if she starts from point 7.

**Ex. 8:** The girl jumps on to the boy's shoulder, finishing in 'swallow'.

The girl stands in the furthest corner of the stage (point 6), facing point 2 on her right foot in *pose croisé devant à terre*. The boy is four to five steps away from her in a diagonal from points 6–2 facing her. The girl runs and *petit assemblé* her right foot and, pressing strongly away from the floor, jumps towards the boy and assumes the 'swallow' whilst in the air with such exactitude that she lands on his left shoulder with both thighs firmly held and still. At the moment when she jumps, the boy places his right hand with palm downwards to hold the girl over her waist; then with a small bend of his knees, he brings his left shoulder forwards and curves his left arm under her thighs. When he has caught her, and ONLY THEN, must he stretch his legs.

In later studies, as the boy brings his left arm forwards, he goes into a turn half clockwise towards point 2. The girl should practise moving from a run and pressing herself off the floor with one foot, that is from a *pas sissonne*.

During all the first studies of this particular lift, the boy must start facing the girl. If she is afraid as she finishes, she should place her left hand over his left.

**Ex. 9:** *Saut de basque* on to the boy's chest.

The girl stands in 2nd *arabesque à terre* on her left foot facing point 1; the boy is three to four steps behind her in the same pose. The girl: *pas chassé* into *saut de basque* in such a direction and with such precision that the movement finishes with her 'sitting' on the boy's chest. The difference between the *saut de basque* of a solo dance and in a lift is that in the lift the girl must NOT brush the left foot too strongly upwards because she must not hit her partner. At the momment of the girl's jump, the boy must bend both knees a little and open his arms sideways as he takes a step forwards to catch the girl on his chest as she takes flight. His right arm is on her waist and his left on her left thigh; he could also hold her waist. Her pose, and the position of the arms are the same as for the lift on the chest, i.e., in 3rd.

**Ex. 10:** *Saut de basque* on to the boy's shoulder.

The preparation is the same as in the preceding example. The girl's problem is to jump a little higher than before because she must aim for the boy's shoulder. During her jump, he must present his right shoulder and straighten carefully without displacing any of her weight. In this version, the boy must catch the girl with both hands on her waist.

**Ex. 11:** Jump on to the boy's shoulder, finishing in the 'sitting' position – sketch 82.

82. Jump on to the partner's shoulder finishing in the 'sitting' position

The girl stands with her back to point 2 on her left foot, *pose croisé devant à terre*. The boy faces her from three to four steps away in 4th position, left foot *croisé devant*. (The position is larger than usual, and his centre of balance must be firmly fixed over his left foot.) The position must NOT be turned-out. His right arm is stretched forwards and his left is to the side. Both arms must be at shoulder level, palms up. The girl: *pas couru* on right and strongly pressing the left on the floor, jumps on to the boy's right shoulder, raising both arms to 3rd. It is essential to sit fully on his shoulder, the left hip pressed against the boy's neck, spine absolutely stretched and vertical, but slightly turned from the waist upwards towards the boy's head. As the girl jumps, the boy must slightly bend his knees and, without pulling his right shoulder backwards, offer it and catch the girl as she 'flies' through the air.

## VARIOUS WAYS OF CHANGING INTO AND OUT OF 'FISH' WHEN RESTING ON THE BOY'S SHOULDER

**Ex. 1:** The girl changes into 'fish' from the 'sitting' position.

The girl is sitting on the boy's right shoulder. His left arm supports her right side and holds her waist between his fingers and thumb, his right hand is on her right hip holding her upright. The girl then stretches her right leg forwards, and, making a *grand rond de jambe*, takes the 'fish' facing point 7. The boy must change his grip as he lowers her.

Such examples of changes when the girl is on the boy's shoulder should be studied with the boy turning a full circle *en place*. On the technical side of double-work it is very important that the change of pose takes place when the boy has his back to point 1.

**Ex. 2:** *The girl changes into 'fish' with a turn in the air.*

The girl is sitting on the boy's right shoulder, see sketch 82, her legs behind his back. The boy, with a short bend and stretch of his knees, slightly throws her upwards. At this signal, the girl swiftly turns her body with the right shoulder forwards and, bending strongly to the left, changes into 'fish' facing point 7. Without allowing her to descend, the boy stretches his left arm round her body and, with the right, draws the girl's right thigh upwards.

Before 'throwing' the girl upwards and round, the boy must stretch upwards on both legs.

**Ex. 3:** *The girl changes from 'fish' to 'swallow' on the boy's shoulder with a turn.*

The girl is in 'fish' facing point 3 in the boy's arms. With a slight bend of his knees, he 'throws' her upwards, simultaneously turning her towards himself with both arms. At the moment of being 'thrown' the girl must energetically help the turn, swiftly raising her arms to 3rd and lifting the body upwards and then taking 'swallow' on the boy's left shoulder. She makes this movement in the same way as she would in *fouetté en tournant*, i.e., the girl's right foot, which is bent at the knee, must be swiftly straightened into 5th position and then both legs simultaneously bent at the knee in order to arrive in the 'swallow'.

Immediately after the girl's legs are straightened, the boy, with a slight bend of his knees, guides his left shoulder forwards, placing the palm of his right hand over the girl's waist and his left under both her hips as support. Resting her on his shoulder, he turns to face point 8. If the teacher is afraid of any accident during training, he should stand facing the boy and place his hand under the girl's body.

## LIFTS AND HOLDS IN GRAND ELEVATION WITH THROWS AND FIXED POSES ON FULL STRETCHED ARMS, WITH AND WITHOUT TURNS IN THE AIR

The principles underlying the work of the boy lifting the girl in the air with both hands either *en place* or with a run are as follows: the boy bends both knees and gives the first impetus by stretching them to the fullest extent; then, as he swiftly lifts the girl upwards, he immediately slightly bends again but completes the lift on fully stretched legs. Thus the greater part of the strain of lifting depends on the strength and accurate movement of the boy's leg muscles.

The girl must be centred exactly over the boy's head when she is finally 'fixed' at the full length and height of his arms. In order to achieve this, at the moment she is lifted he must make a short step as if to get below her body, but he must in no way slacken at the waist, as this often leads to spinal injury. The teacher must insist that the boy accomplishes the lift with the correct placing of the body.

As a rule, during lessons the girl, after a lift, should return to the floor in *demi-plié* in order to avoid injury to her knee-joints.

These difficult lifts and 'throws' with the girl are not necessarily studied in all classes. The teacher must discriminate and assess the physical capacity of each boy, his professional expertise, and physical aptitude.

## GRAND ELEVATION WITH BOTH ARMS HOLDING THE GIRL'S BODY

**Ex. 1:** *Grand jeté* in 1st *arabesque* – sketch 83.

The girl stands in 5th position, her left foot *devant*, arms in the preparatory position. The boy is behind her near to her right shoulder, both hands on her waist. With a *demi-plié* and *glissade* starting right foot and without change, the girl strongly presses out of the floor from the left foot into *grand jeté* in 1st *arabesque* towards point 3. She must jump upwards only and not throw her body forwards. The boy, without leaving go her waist, and as she does *glissade*, lightly changes the line of his hands on her waist, the left slightly backwards towards and under her left shoulder blade, his right slightly forwards. He must also direct the fingers of both hands upwards.

As the girl jumps, the boy swiftly moves to lift her above himself by stretching both arms upwards; not allowing himself to move forwards, so that he can softly lower the girl to the floor in *fondu*. Alternatively, he could allow himself one or two paces as he catches her, thus giving the audience the illusion of a longer flight.

It is very important that the trajectory of the girl's flight in the air completes an even half circle.

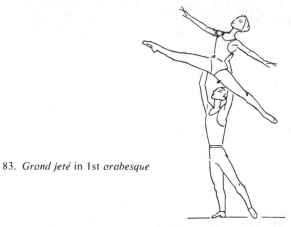

83. *Grand jeté* in 1st *arabesque*

**Ex. 2:** *Grand jeté en tournant en attitude* – sketch 84.

The girl stands in *attitude croisée à terre* on her left foot. The boy is behind her, both hands on her waist. Girl: *fondu* into *pas glissade*, right foot, and, pushing away from the floor, with her left moves into *grand jeté en tournant en attitude*. The boy moves simultaneously with the girl in *pas glissade* (a little further than the girl) and changes the line of his hands on her waist, the left a little upwards towards her left shoulder blade and the right along her waist.

As the girl jumps, he swiftly stretches both arms, lifting and directing her towards point 8. He then transfers the central weight of her body from the left to his right arm and lowers her softly to the floor on her right foot *fondu* in *attitude croisée*. During the lift, the boy adopts the basic principles for the action of the palms of the hands. The girl MUST JUMP UPWARDS ONLY and without thrusting her body forwards.

84. *Grand jeté en tournant* in *attitude*

**Ex. 3:** *Grand pas de basque.*

The girl stands in 5th position, right foot *devant*, arms in preparatory position. The boy is behind her, both hands on her waist. Girl: *pas glissade* commencing right foot and, without changing, *coupé* left foot into *grand pas de basque* turning towards point 2. As she does *pas glissade*, the boy changes the line of his hands on her body so that the heels of his hands are pressed together, but his fingers embrace the body. As the girl jumps, she allows her body to curve backwards at the shoulders a little further than she would in a solo dance so that she receives support from the boy's arm.

At the same moment as the girl jumps, the boy, drawing her towards himself, carries her in the direction of the jump, i.e., towards point 2, and then lowers her to the floor softly in *demi-plié*.

*Grand pas de chat* is performed in the same way.

**Ex. 4:** *Jeté entrelacé* partners facing each other – sketch 85.

The girl stands with her back to point 7 on her left foot *pose croisé derrière à terre*. The boy faces her about one step away in any pose suggested by the teacher. Commencing with her right foot, the girl steps and then moves into *jeté élancé* along a straight line from point 7–3, placing both hands firmly on both the boy's shoulders. She must jump so that her hands are placed just over the top of his shoulders; also so that the centre of her weight is placed exactly over the boy's central line of balance. During the jump, her head must be inclined slightly backwards.

85. *Jeté entrelacé* (partners facing each other)

The boy holds both hands on her body so that they are on top of her hips, but during the lift he must change the position of his wrists very slightly so that his fingers move upwards a little to hold her waist very firmly.

As the girl jumps, the boy must take a small step forwards in order to get below her body as he lifts her above his head. He simultaneously turns towards point 3 as he steps, and lowers her softly to the floor in *demi-plié*.

# LIFTS IN A FIXED POSITION ON FULLY STRETCHED ARMS

**Ex. 1:** *Lifting the girl holding her under her waist* – sketch 86.

The girl stands in 5th position, right foot *devant*, arms in preparatory position. The boy is behind her, hands on her waist. Girl: *demi-plié* and jump upwards raising arms to 3rd. Having reached the highest point, she bends her body backwards from waist and shoulder girdle. As the girl jumps, the boy lifts her by slightly bending his knees then walking one step forwards in order to get under her body, as he simultaneously places his hands under her waist so that the heels of his palms are pressed together and the tips of the fingers of both hands hold her waist.

During the return to the floor, the girl must straighten her body and finish in 5th position *demi-plié*.

86. Lift holding the girl beneath her waist

**Ex. 2:** *Lifting the girl in* 1st *arabesque en place* – sketch 87.

In most theatrical practice, lifting the girl into the air is usually performed on the right hand side (that is considered the basic principle) because the left side, owing to the position of the heart, must not encounter too much strain or pressure. Moreover, it is not usual to study working on the left side, nor with the boy's left arm, because it is usually weaker than the right, even though the boy may be left-handed.

The girl is in 1st *arabesque* on right *pointe*. The boy is behind her, both hands on her body. Feeling that the girl is strongly steady, he takes a half step forwards on his right foot, bends his knees slightly, and draws his right hand under her diaphragm (a little nearer the right side than the left) and places his left hand under her left thigh. His hands must be at the same level and the width of his shoulders apart, palms upwards, fingers widely stretched longways, holding the girl equally on both right and left hands.

The girl: *fondu* on her right *pointe* and strongly push off, the right foot upwards from the floor at the same time as the boy lifts her and stabilises her pose on high. During the lift, she bends her right knee and allows the right toe to rest in the centre of her left (lower) leg.

87. Lift of 1st *arabesque en place*

It is very important that the girl holds her 1st *arabesque* strongly at the moment when she is lifted from the floor. She must ON NO ACCOUNT incline her body forwards, nor slacken the working leg.

To lower the girl to the floor, the boy must allow her to reach his chest before bending his knees. At this moment, she stretches her right leg and, as her toe reaches the floor, gradually sink into *fondu* by which time she will be holding her own weight.

This lift should not frighten any girl as long as she maintains her pose. Any who are afraid should be helped by someone holding her left arm and another her right.

The lift can also be studied at the beginning by lifting the girl only as far as the chest.

**Ex. 3:** *Lifting the girl in 3rd arabesque* – sketch 88.

The girl stands with her back to point 7; the boy faces her three to four steps away in a straight line between points 7–3. The poses are arranged by the teacher. The girl runs and, without passing the boy, *sissonne tombée* on her left foot, strongly pushing into and immediately out of the floor, jumps upwards in 3rd *arabesque* towards point 3.

It is important that before the lift, the boy's hands are absolutely at the same level. Also, the girl's right leg when she jumps must be

88. Lift in 3rd *arabesque*

stretched out fully and not above 100° from the floor. If it is any higher, she and he will find it difficult to catch and hold the pose in the air. She must jump as if to go above the boy and not 'fly' over him. The palm of his right hand must be so placed that his fingers point slightly upwards. The left hand is also opened palm up, but his fingers stretched downwards. As the girl does *sissonne tombée*, he must stretch both arms forwards and, bending his knees, place his right hand on her hip and his left hand about the middle of her right thigh; see sketch 87. He immediately steps forwards and lifts her as he stabilises her pose in 3rd *arabesque* with his arms stretched to their fullest. During the lift the boy MUST NOT ALLOW his right shoulder to move backwards.

During the first study of this lift in 3rd *arabesque*, it is advisable NOT to allow the girl to bend her left leg up to her right, but to leave it stretched downwards.

The teacher will find it useful to stand behind the boy and hold the girl's two hands if the boy collapses. If the girl misjudges her distance, the same presence would help.

**Ex. 4:** *Lifting the girl in 4th arabesque with grand fouetté sauté –* sketch 89.

Lifts in 4th *arabesque* should firstly be studied without a jump and using exactly the same principles as used when lifting the girl in 1st *arabesque*.

The girl stands in 1st *arabesque* facing point 2. The boy is about two steps behind her in a diagonal between points 2–6 in the same or another pose. The girl: *pas glissade* towards the boy, then strongly push the left foot out of the floor into *grand fouetté*, finishing in 4th *arabesque*. She must JUMP UPWARDS ONLY. She must 'fly' over her partner and NOT PAST HIM. The pose of 4th *arabesque* in the air must be absolutely correct and will depend entirely on her control over her body and its direction. The boy catches and lifts her at that moment when her jump in *grand fouetté* has turned into 4th *arabesque*. His right hand must find the girl's right side and his left

76

the centre of her right thigh. When lowering the girl to the floor, he again bends his elbows and lowers her to chest level. Only then does he bend his knees to allow her to sink to the floor in 4th *arabesque fondu*.

If the teacher is afraid that the lift will not succeed, he should stand about one step away facing the boy and hold the girl's torso with his left hand.

The preparatory jump in most lifts is more like a *grand temps levé* or *sissonne* in 4th *arabesque*, because at the moment of 'flight' the girl must be in 4th *arabesque* and MUST NOT TURN in the boy's arms whilst performing a *grand fouetté*. If she does, she will slip through his arms.

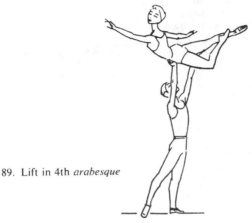

89. Lift in 4th *arabesque*

**Ex. 5:** *Lifting the girl in 'swallow' from a run* – sketch 90.

The girl stands back to point 7 on her right foot *pose croisé devant à terre*. The boy faces her back to point 3 from five to six steps away along a straight line between points 7–3. Girl: *pas couru* towards the boy and without passing him, falls into *pas tombé* on her left foot, strongly pressing out of the floor and being lifted in 'swallow'. As the girl jumps, both her hips must be on an exact level with the boy's shoulders. She must gauge her run and jump so that she does not 'fly' past him, but jump as if to go over him. As the girl does *sissonne tombé*, the boy bends his knees slightly, and places both his hands on her hips so that the strain of holding her weight firmly rests on the heels of the palms of his hands. His fingers must rest on the front of the girl's lower ribs. As she jumps, he lifts her and stabilizes her 'swallow' at the fullest stretch of his arms.

Whenever the girl finishes a pose with the body held in a finely stretched curve from the head to the toes, she must NEVER allow her spine or head to drop forwards, otherwise there will be an accident.

The best way to lower the girl to the floor from this lift is as follows: the boy bends his elbows and lowers the girl to his chest level. At the same time, she stretches her right (lower) leg downwards and then he bends his knees to place her softly on the floor in *fondu* or *demi-plié*.

If the teacher is afraid that the lift will not succeed, he must stand about one step away from the boy's back and, if there is a mishap, catch the girl by her arms or her shoulder.

When the girl studies the 'swallow' using fully stretched legs and curving body backwards as an exercise in student's work, she must not consider it as an acrobatic feat, but as a small part of the regular repertoire of the classical dancer.

**Ex. 6:** Lifting the girl in *saut de basque*, finishing in the 'sitting' position on the boy's fully stretched arms – sketch 91.

The girl stands facing point 2 on her left foot, in 2nd *arabesque à terre*. The boy is behind her from three to four steps away in the same pose. Girl: *pas chassé* towards the boy and into *saut de basque* with such accuracy that the jump finishes on a level with his chest in the 'sitting' position. N.B. Always begin teaching this lift by insisting the girl must jump to this level.

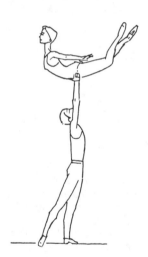 

90. 'Swallow' at the highest stretch of the partner's arms

91. 'Sitting' at the highest stretch of the partner's arms

As the girl does her *saut de basque*, the boy bends his knee slightly and takes a step backwards on his right foot, placing his hands on her buttocks and lifts her, thus stabilizing her 'sitting' position on fully stretched arms.

Again, it is essential to lift the girl to chest level and only when this position is assured must the boy practise stretching his arms to their fullest. To lower the girl to the floor, the boy follows the preceding instructions.

If the teacher is afraid that the lift will fail, he must stand behind the boy about one step away and, in case of misjudgement, catch the girl with two hands on her waist.

**Ex. 7:** The girl finishes *grand jeté* in 1st *arabesque* on the boy's fully stretched arms.

Girl: *pas glissade* commencing right foot and pushing strongly out of the floor with the left into *grand jeté* in 1st *arabesque* towards point 3. The boy sharply lifts her with his right hand, and quickly places his left hand beneath her left hip, thus stabilizing her position in 1st *arabesque* at the highest possible stretch of his arms.

To achieve the true height of this lift, the girl must transfer her weight slightly forwards on to the boy's right arm so that his left hand has a brief moment to change its position to under her left thigh.

If the teacher is afraid that this lift will be mistimed, he should face the direction of the lift and place his left hand under the girl's torso and move simultaneously with the lift and brief transfer of weight.

Other examples should be studied, the girl using *grand jeté en attitude effacée.*

## LIFTS WITH FIXED POSES ON THE FULLEST STRETCH OF THE BOY'S ARMS

Without any exception, all the lifts in fixed poses on one hand take place with the active participation of the boy's other hand. The positions are explained in each exercise. The study of such exercises must only proceed when the students are able absolutely to co-ordinate their movements with those of their partners.

**Ex. 1:** *Lifting the girl by holding her under her waist* – sketch 92.

The girl stands in 5th position *sur les pointes*, right foot *devant*, arms in *arabesque*. The boy is behind her, hands on her waist. Girl: bend left knee not too turned-out, the toe resting just behind the right calf. The boy all but kneels on his right knee and places his right hand on the centre of her body, his first finger and thumb stretched open along the waist line, palm fully flattened against the pelvis. His left hand is placed just below the girl's left knee.

92. One hand lift under the girl's waist

Girl: *fondu* and jump upwards, strongly pushing away from the floor with the right foot. At this moment, the boy lifts her with both arms and when his right arm is fully stretched at the elbow, the girl smoothly bends backwards from her waist and shoulder girdle. This allows the boy to hold her with one hand. The boy then stretches his left arm into 2nd, and the girl remains firmly stabilized on his right arm. She then stretches her left leg downwards to join the right in 5th position. Note carefully that the girl's left leg, bent at the knee, must be held absolutely FIRM and still during the lift, in order to allow the boy to use both arms.

The best way to lower the girl to the floor is as follows: the boy places his left hand round and towards the left side of the girl's waist as she smoothly straightens her body into the perpendicular. Once he has the girl in both arms, he lowers her softly to the floor in *demi-plié*.

The artistic quality of this lift depends entirely upon its smoothness. Throughout, the boy must keep his right hand firmly fixed on the girl's waist and his left just below her left knee. As she jumps, she must strongly stretch her left leg downwards as if she wants to step on it; in this way she definitely helps her partner and makes the lift look and feel lighter.

If the teacher is afraid of any mishap, he should stand by the boy's right shoulder and place his left hand on the girl's waist.

**Ex. 2:** *Lifting the girl in sitting position* – sketch 93.

The preparation is the same as in the preceding example. The boy then bends his knees deeply and places his left hand just below the girl's left knee and the palm of his right hand under her buttocks. The girl, *sur les pointes*, does *fondu* and pushes herself strongly from the floor to jump upwards. At this moment, the boy lifts her with both arms and then leaves go with his left hand to hold the girl firmly on the right hand in the 'sitting' position. During the lift, the girl must hold her body absolutely strong and still from the waist upwards. shoulders held down and the pelvic muscles drawn together.

93. 'Sitting' on the partner's hand: 3 poses

The girl should be lowered to the floor as follows: the boy takes the girl's left knee in his left hand and lowers her to chest level; then bends deeply to place her on the floor on one foot.

The girl, whilst still 'sitting' on one hand, usually straightens her left leg, bringing it into the air in 5th position. The boy then places his left hand on her diaphragm and lowers her to the floor on two feet.

In other examples, the boy can lower the girl on to his chest, where she changes into 'fish' facing point 7. He then places his left arm below her waist and holds her right thigh upwards with his right hand. This lift can also be performed by 'throwing' the girl into the air during the change of pose.

**Ex. 3:** The girl's *saut de basque* finishes 'sitting' on the boy's hand.

The girl stands facing point 8 on her left foot, the right *pointe tendue derrière à terre* on a diagonal towards point 4, her right arm in 3rd position and her left in 2nd. The boy is behind her about three to four steps away in the same diagonal and pose. Girl: short *pas chassé* with right into *saut de basque* making a three-quarter turn in the air with such precision that she rises to the height of the boy's chest in 'sitting' position. In this case, her left side will descend on to his chest. As the girl does *pas chassé*, the boy must deeply bend both knees and, when she turns her left side towards him, catch her with his right hand under her buttocks, his left hand under her left knee.

The girl's jump lightens the lift, and the pose must be absolutely stabilised when the boy releases his left hand.

If the teacher fears problems, he should stand behind and by the boy's right shoulder.

The return to the floor is the same as in the preceding examples.

**Ex. 4:** *Grand jeté* into *attitude éffacée* on the boy's arm – sketch 94.

The girl stands with her back to point 4 on her left foot in *pose croisé devant à terre*. The boy is behind her and by her left shoulder, right hand on her right side (near the bottom of her right shoulder blade). He holds the girl's left hand in his left, palm to palm. His feet are in the same position as the girl's. Girl: *glissade* into *grand jeté*

94. *Jeté* in *attitude éffaceé*, one hand on the waist

*en attitude éffacée* diagonally towards point 8. The boy does *glissade* with her, leading her with his left hand, elbow bent, and held near her left hip. As the girl jumps, he lifts her with both hands. She pushes herself upwards by pressing her left hand on his left, but without raising her shoulders. She must arch her back strongly as well as her shoulder girdle. Only the boy's right arm takes the weight of the girl's body and, when it is stabilised, he immediately opens his left arm to the side. When first studying this lift, the boy should not relinquish the girl's hand and NEVER push her arm upwards: SHE MUST DO THAT.

The girl's return to the floor can be as follows: the boy again takes the girl's left hand and brings it towards her hip. She, without straightening her body, joins her feet in 5th position. The boy, bending his knees, places both arms round the girl and, as she straightens, lowers her to the floor in *demi-plié*.

In other variations of this lift, the boy can place his left hand on the girl's diaphragm and when she finishes her jump she can then move into *attitude* or stretch to 1st or 2nd *arabesque*.

If the teacher is afraid that the lift will be mistimed, he should stand behind the boy, and if necessary place his hands under the girl's back.

## 'THROWING' THE GIRL INTO THE AIR WITH AND WITHOUT A CHANGE OF POSE

Before 'throwing' the girl into the air (from a stabilized pose) from his fully stretched arms, the boy must make a quick *plié*, keeping his body absolutely straight, his arm fully stretched; then quickly stretch his knees just after he has caught the girl.

**Ex. 1:** 'Throwing' the girl from 1st *arabesque* to 'fish'.

The girl is held in the air in 1st *arabesque* in the boy's arms facing point 3. The boy bends his knees slightly and 'throws' the girl straight upwards and then catches her in 'fish' with his right arm under her body and his left over her left thigh.

In this lift, the girl must move accurately as she changes and in no way stiffen. The boy cushions her change by stretching his legs. His body must remain absolutely straight.

If the teacher is afraid that the lift will be mistimed, he should stand facing the boy and place his left hand under the girl's torso.

**Ex. 2:** Throwing the girl from 1st *arabesque* into 'fish' with a turn of the body.

This lift is taken from 1st *arabesque* as above (in the air). Both begin, the boy 'throwing' the girl slightly upwards whereupon she immediately joins her legs together in 5th position whilst raising her arms in 3rd, turning to bring the right shoulder to the front and moving into 'fish' facing point 7. The boy places his left arm under her body and his right over her right thigh. In moving from one pose to the other the girl must not sit on the boy's chest. Her hip must at all times be strongly directed forwards, her body held strongly at the waist and shoulder girdle, her head stretched up and backwards.

**Ex. 3:** 'Throwing' the girl from 3rd *arabesque* into 'fish' with a turn of the body.

The girl is already in 3rd *arabesque*, held high. Both are facing point 8 so that the girl brings her left shoulder backwards towards the boy as he throws her straight upwards. She makes a full turn in the horizontal position and falls into 'fish', facing point 3. Before the turn, her left arm quickly moves into 3rd position and her feet must close in 5th for a second whilst in the air. After the turn, she bends her right knee and allows the toe to rest on the centre of the left ankle. The boy catches her with his right arm under her body and his left under her left thigh.

**Ex. 4:** 'Throwing' the girl from 4th *arabesque* into 'fish' with a small turn in the air.

Both begin facing point 8, the girl high in 4th *arabesque*. The boy 'throws' the girl up lightly; at this moment she must stretch her legs into 5th position for a moment and raise her arms to 3rd, just turning her body to the left, and assume the 'fish' facing point 3. In this case the boy must throw the girl upwards more strongly, but catch her in the same way as above.

**Ex. 5:** *'Throwing' the girl from 'swallow' into 'fish' with a full turn.*

The girl is in 'swallow' on the boy's left shoulder; see sketch 78. The boy lightly throws the girl straight upwards. At this moment, she makes a full turn to the right, moving into the horizontal position, joining her feet in 5th and raising her arms to 3rd. After the turn she assumes 'fish' facing point 3. The boy catches her with his right arm under her body and places his left hand over her thighs.

**Ex. 6:** Double *tour en l'air* in the horizontal position ('double fish') sketch 95.

It is important in classical *pas de deux* that the girl uses three jumps: *jeté entrelacé*, which helps her to throw her body into the horizontal position; and the 'force' for a *tour en l'air* is taken as in *assemblé en tournant*, are two of them. Both are used here.

95. 'Double fish' (the moment of flight into the turn

The girl is in 1st *arabesque* (high) on her right *pointe*; the boy is three to four steps away from her in a straight line between points 3–7 in the same pose, but *à terre*. Girl: *pas chassé* towards boy, *tombé* on left foot and brush right towards point 7 rising in the air into the horizontal position. She joins her left foot to her right and raises her arms to 3rd. She must judge her preparation and jump so that her hips are in front of the boy's chest, and so that she takes 'force' for the turn at the highest point of her flight. The boy places both hands on her waist and 'throws' her strongly upwards as he gives 'impetus' for the turn to her left side, i.e., towards himself. His right hand is slightly above her waist and towards her right shoulder blade – this helps to keep the girl in the horizontal position. His left hand reaches above her body towards her right hip, because he must actively 'throw' her upwards and give 'impetus' to her turn with his hand.

After a double turn in the air in the horizontal position, the girl goes into 'fish' as he catches her body with his right hand and her left thigh with his left hand.

This lift demands absolute co-ordination of movement and tempo from both boy and girl; therefore it requires more practice than any other lift.